# Suffering and the Intelligence of Love in the Teaching Life

Sean Steel · Amber Homeniuk
Editors

# Suffering and the Intelligence of Love in the Teaching Life

In Light and In Darkness

*Editors*
Sean Steel
Calgary Board of Education
University of Calgary
Calgary, AB, Canada

Amber Homeniuk
Ontario, ON, Canada

ISBN 978-3-030-05957-6      ISBN 978-3-030-05958-3  (eBook)
https://doi.org/10.1007/978-3-030-05958-3

Library of Congress Control Number: 2018968270

© The Editor(s) (if applicable) and The Author(s) 2019
This work is subject to copyright. All rights are solely and exclusively licensed by the Publisher, whether the whole or part of the material is concerned, specifically the rights of translation, reprinting, reuse of illustrations, recitation, broadcasting, reproduction on microfilms or in any other physical way, and transmission or information storage and retrieval, electronic adaptation, computer software, or by similar or dissimilar methodology now known or hereafter developed.
The use of general descriptive names, registered names, trademarks, service marks, etc. in this publication does not imply, even in the absence of a specific statement, that such names are exempt from the relevant protective laws and regulations and therefore free for general use.
The publisher, the authors and the editors are safe to assume that the advice and information in this book are believed to be true and accurate at the date of publication. Neither the publisher nor the authors or the editors give a warranty, express or implied, with respect to the material contained herein or for any errors or omissions that may have been made. The publisher remains neutral with regard to jurisdictional claims in published maps and institutional affiliations.

Cover credit: © Sylvia Steel

This Palgrave Macmillan imprint is published by the registered company Springer Nature Switzerland AG
The registered company address is: Gewerbestrasse 11, 6330 Cham, Switzerland

*For Patch Adams:*

*Thank you for writing both to me and to my students, and I hope that this book begins to address what you have called the need for "the intelligence of love."*

# Acknowledgements

As the editors of this book, we would like to thank Milana Vernikova, Linda Braus, and the people at Palgrave Macmillan for providing us with the opportunity to assemble all of these writings for publication, and especially for their support in affirming the value of this important topic in the field of education. We would also like to express to each of our fine authors how thankful we are that they entrusted their thoughtful work into our hands, that they were willing to come together and to share their many and diverse perspectives on suffering in a common space for consideration and dialogue, as well as our gratitude for the patience they have shown while we have worked diligently over these past months (and now years!) to navigate all the difficult challenges of bringing a project with so many moving parts to light. Thanks to all of you.

# Contents

**Elemental**   1
Keith Inman

**Chapter 1: Introduction—In Light and In Darkness**   3
Sean Steel and Amber Homeniuk

**Part I   Analyses of the Meaning of Suffering in Teaching**

**Plato killed a moth in my dream**   21
Daniela Elza

**Chapter 2: Suffering and the Contemplative Gaze in Teaching**   23
Sean Steel

**Chapter 3: On the Two Meanings of Suffering**   37
James V. Schall

Part II  Suffering and the Long View: Wisdom Through Experience

Oh, my dark companion ...                                49
John B. Lee

Chapter 4: Caring for Humanity                           53
Sandra Ens

Chapter 5: I Can't Believe It Myself Most Days ...       59
John B. Lee

Part III  East-Meets-West: Finding Rhythms and Articulating Meaning in Suffering

ode to the critic (or what was I trying to say?)         69
Daniela Elza

Chapter 6: Suffering and the Blues                       73
Harry Manx

*it:* attempts at definition                             79
Daniela Elza

Chapter 7: Ajahn Chah Gives a Teaching                   83
Tim Ward

Part IV  Teaching, Limitations, and Marginalization in Suffering

Chapter 8: The Give-Back of the Giving                   93
Kelley Aitken

**Chapter 9: Teaching Tiny Tim from My Tiny Tim Closet—A Personal Essay**     99
Dorothy Ellen Palmer

**Chapter 10: Making Space—It's Okay to Clear Time for Yourself**     111
Jenna Butler

**Part V    Suffering Spiritual Tensions and the Pursuit of Wisdom in Teaching**

**Importance**     117
Keith Inman

**Chapter 11: A Teacher's Night Song**     119
Sean Steel

**a shoreline to stand on**     133
Daniela Elza

**Chapter 12: "Living in the Shadow of What I Teach," or Rather, "Learning from Our Needs"**     135
Stefan Gillow Reynolds

**Part VI    Suffering, Joy, and Gratitude in Teaching**

**beauty is embarrassing**     151
Daniela Elza

**Chapter 13: Never Quite Enough**     155
Tom Flanagan

**Chapter 14: Why Students Don't Suffer**     159
Lee Trepanier

**The Drawing Lesson** 183
Kelley Aitken

**Chapter 16: A Time to Weep and a Time to Laugh, Or, the
Necessity of Suffering Even As We Live Happily Ever After** 187
Dorothy Warner

**Chapter 17: Once in a Blue Moon** 195
Christina Alise McDermott

**Index** 199

# Notes on Contributors

**Kelley Aitken** is a writer and artist. *Canadian Shield*, a collection of short stories informed by the Canadian wilderness was launched by Tightrope books in June of 2016 and earned an IPPY (Independent Publishers Prize of the Year) bronze medallion for fiction, Canada East Region. Her earlier collection, *Love in a Warm Climate*, The Porcupine's Quill, '98 was nominated for the Commonwealth Prize, Best First Book, Canadian Caribbean Region. She is the co-editor of the anthology *First Writes*, The Banff Press, '05. With Maureen Scott Harris, she launched "The Raven and the Writing Desk" in 2007, a chapbook of Maureen's haiku and Kelley's wash drawings. She teaches drawing and painting at the Art Gallery of Ontario, the Aga Khan Museum and co-leads *plein air* painting groups to France. She is currently working on a collection of essays about drawing and museum space. An excerpt: "A Tree, an Elephant, Departure" was published as a chapbook by Field Notes, in 2015.

**Jenna Butler** teaches in the areas of creative writing (poetry and fiction) and ecocriticism. Her research interests include creative writing pedagogy, ecosemiotics, and ecotranslatology. She is the author of three books of poetry, *Seldom Seen Road*, *Wells*, and *Aphelion*, and a collection of ecological essays, *On the Grizzly Trail*. She is the editor of over thirty collections of fiction and poetry for presses in Canada and England, including five titles for Alberta's NeWest Press.

Butler has published several scholarly articles and chapters, with upcoming essays in new books on Canadian poet Robert Kroetsch

(Guernica Writers Series) and British poets Denise Riley and Liz Berry (Eyewear Press). She has presented papers on poetry and ecocriticism at conferences in England, Tenerife, Canada, and the States, and her work as a writer in residence has taken her from Ireland to the Arctic Circle. Butler is the recipient of the Canadian Authors Association Exporting Alberta Award and a Lieutenant Governor of Alberta Arts Award. She was a 2014 YWCA Women of Distinction nominee as an educator.

**Daniela Elza's** work has appeared inter/nationally in over 100 publications. Her poetry collections are *The Weight of Dew* (2012), *The Book of It* (2011), and *Milk Tooth Bane Bone* (2013), of which David Abram says: "Out of the ache of the present moment, Daniela Elza has crafted something spare and irresistible, an open armature for wonder." Daniela earned her doctorate in Philosophy of Education from Simon Fraser University (2011). She lives and writes in Vancouver, Canada.

**Sandra Ens, B.Ed., Dip. Ed, M.A.** taught high school English for 33 years, until her retirement in 2013. Sandra has taught at a number of schools surrounding Calgary. Sandra became actively involved in the Professional Development arm of the Alberta Teachers Association, organizing opportunities for veteran teachers, and mentoring novice teachers and practicum students. She served as local president for four years. Retirement has allowed more time for gardening, travel, exercise, and completing the NYT Crossword Puzzle every day.

**Tom Flanagan** is Professor Emeritus of political science at the University of Calgary. He started teaching in 1968 and retired in 2013, but still teaches one course a year in the Master of Public Policy Programme. He is best known for his research on aboriginal issues and for his work as campaign manager for conservative political parties. He is a Fellow of the Royal Society of Canada.

**Amber Homeniuk's** writing appears in The Malahat Review, The Fiddlehead, Numéro Cinq, and Windsor Review's tribute to Alice Munro. Amber's poems are anthologized in Beyond the Seventh Morning (SandCrab, 2012), *Window Fishing: The Night We Caught Beatlemania* (Hidden Brook, 2013), and Best Canadian Poetry in English (Tightrope Books, 2016). Her first chapbook is *Product of Eden: Field of Mice* (Norfolk Arts Centre, 2013). In 2015 she was a finalist in the PRISM International Poetry Contest, shortlisted for the Montreal International Poetry Prize, and won Readers' Choice for Arc's Poem of the Year. Intimately acquainted with suffering via both her personal experience of multiple chronic illnesses and her profession, Amber lives in rural southwestern Ontario, works as an expressive arts therapist, blogs groovy outfits at Butane Anvil, and is kept by a small flock of hens.

**Keith Inman** is an internationally published, award-winning poet. His book, *The War Poems: Screaming at Heaven* from Black Moss Press 2014, earned strong reviews for poetry about "the common experiences of people ... touched by war" (Canlit #223). Keith lives in an old stone home overlooking the Welland Canal in Ontario, Canada. His new book of poetry, a story of loss and redemption through the eyes of a young interracial couple, is forthcoming from Black Moss Press.

**John B. Lee** was a secondary school teacher of English, Creative Writing, and Dramatic Arts at Waterford District High School from 1974 to 1989. Since then he has lectured at university, served as writer in residence, and mentored writers of all ages and at all stages of their careers from beginners through advanced published professionals. In 2005, he was named Poet Laureate of the city of Brantford in perpetuity, and in 2016 Poet Laureate of Norfolk County for life. The recipient of over eighty prestigious writing awards, his work has appeared internationally in over five hundred publications and he is the author of nearly one hundred books. He lives in a lake house on the shores of Long Point Bay in Port Dover where he works as a full-time author.

**Harry Manx** was born on the Isle of Man (UK) and immigrated to Canada as a child. Raised on hockey and rock and roll in southern Ontario he became a roadie for bands in the early 70s eventually landing a job as a sound tech in the famed El Macombo club in Toronto. There he witnessed the Blues close up and felt inspired to play the slide guitar. For the next twenty-five years, he busked his way around the globe spending time in Europe, Japan, Brazil, and India.

For a dozen years, he lived and studied music in India with a Master musician (VM Bhatt) learning to play a hybrid 20-stringed slide guitar called the Mohan Veena. On returning to Canada in 2000 he released his first CD to critical acclaim becoming the "Blues CD of the Year".

Called "the most expressive Blues player in Canada" by *Billboard* magazine and described as "being one of a kind" by *Downbeat* magazine, Harry has made his own unique mark on the world of music. Following up on the first disc, he has released 14 CDs in 14 years, many of which have received awards and nominations. Harry lives on Salt Spring Island in BC with his wife and son.

**Christina Alise McDermott** is a 14-year veteran teacher who started her career teaching Kindergarten to Grade 6 in a two-room school house in Toad River, BC (Mile 422) on the Alaska Highway. Since then, she has taught in a variety of grade configurations, as well as been a Teacher Librarian. She happened upon teaching when she realized that she was awfully close to graduating Simon Fraser University, and really had no idea what she wanted to do with the rest of her life. A friend talked her ear off about how amazing teaching was, and suggested volunteering in a classroom to try it out. On that first day, within the first 30 min she experienced what can only be called a spiritual moment, and realized that she had found her Calling and Home. While Christina's teaching journey has had moments of bliss, there have been other moments of despair and gut-wrenching sorrow. In the end, there is no other career that she would rather be doing.

**Dorothy Ellen Palmer** is a disabled senior writer, binge knitter, Sherlock Holmes fan, mom, retired teacher and improv coach. Like the protagonist of her first novel, *When Fenelon Falls* (Coach House, 2010), she was illicitly conceived during Hurricane Hazel and adopted at age three. She grew up in Alderwood, Toronto, and spent her childhood summers at a three-generation cottage near Fenelon Falls. Over three decades, she worked as a high school English/Drama teacher, teaching on a Mennonite Colony, a four-room school, an Adult Learning Centre attached to a prison, and a highly diverse new high school in Pickering, where she created the only high school improv program in Canada and coached for The Canadian Improv Games. Elected to her union executive each year for fifteen years, she created staff and student workshops to fight bullying, racism, sexism, sexual harassment, and homophobia.

**Dr. Stefan Gillow Reynolds** taught at Georgetown University and London University, he is the author of *Living with the Mind of Christ: Mindfulness in Christian Spirituality* (London: Dart, Longman and Todd, 2016). He is currently Retreat Director of the Mount Melleray Institute for Christian Spirituality in Ireland. He is a Benedictine Oblate of The World Community for Christian Meditation and a lay Associate of the Irish Cistercians.

**James V. Schall, S.J.** is Professor Emeritus, Georgetown University. His most recent books are: *Docilitas: On Teaching and Being Taught*; *The Line through the Human Heart: On Sinning and Being Forgiven*, and *Catholicism and Intelligence*.

**Sean Steel** is a public school teacher who has been a Lecturer and Sessional Instructor at the University of Calgary, Ambrose University College, and the Southern Alberta Institute of Technology. He has published numerous articles in the fields of Education, Law, Religious Studies, and Philosophy. His books include (with Kim Koh and Cecile DePass) *The Good, The Bad, and The Ugly: Developing Teacher's Assessment Literacy Within Cross-Cultural Contexts* (Brill/Sense Publishers, in press), *Teacher Education and the Pursuit of Wisdom: A Practical Guide for Education Philosophy Courses* (Peter Lang, 2018), and *The Pursuit of Wisdom and Happiness in Education: Historical Sources and Contemplative Practices* (SUNY Press, 2014). Sean lives with his family in Calgary, Alberta, along with a dog and a cat.

**Lee Trepanier** is a Professor of Political Science at Saginaw Valley State University; series editor of "Lexington Book's Politics, Literature, and Film"; editor of the academic website, *VoegelinView*; and author and editor of several books, the latest being *The Socratic Method Today* (Routledge, 2018).

**Tim Ward** is the author of six books, including the best-selling *What the Buddha Never Taught* and *Savage Breast: One Man's Search for the Goddess*. His travel stories have appeared in 13 anthologies, including Traveller's Tales *Best Travel Writing 2006, 2010, 2011* and *2012*. Tim is also the publisher of Changemakers Books (an imprint of John Hunt Publishing). He also co-owns Intermedia Communications Training with Teresa Erickson, his wife and business partner.

They live in Maryland.

**Dorothy Warner** is a writer, wife, and mother of four, living in the Washington, DC area. She has worked in the accounting field in the non-profit and for-profit sectors. A former homeschooler and part-time teacher, a current artisanal baker and organic gardener, she writes frequently on family and educational topics.

# Elemental

## *Keith Inman*

A student wanted to know,
why choose poetry

"when you could put all your energy
into a song, or a play, or make
a bundle from a novel?"

Chatter flowed around the room,
rebounded off walls like static, as if,
the reverberations had nowhere specific to go.

I thought of a river
flooding its banks,
carving new channels to the moon

but mentioned that, perhaps, inspiration,
like water or electricity,
followed a path of least resistance.

---

K. Inman (✉)
Thorold, ON, Canada

# Chapter 1:
# Introduction—In Light and In Darkness

*Sean Steel and Amber Homeniuk*

Authors, statesmen, philosophers, poets, artists, musicians, and of course, *teachers* have all long-asked questions about the meaning of human suffering. In his speech upon the occasion of Martin Luther King's assassination, Senator Robert F. Kennedy looked to the ancient poet Aeschylus for a riddled response to this question. Famously, he spoke to the American people, who were full to the brim with nation-wide lamentations, saying: "Even in our sleep, pain, which cannot forget, falls drop by drop upon the heart, until, in our own despair, against our will, comes wisdom through the awful grace of God."[1] Most often, when we speak or think about human suffering and the illumination of its meaning in our lives, we rely upon images of light and darkness. Consider, for instance, Giordano Bruno's sixteenth century description of the turmoil-filled soul's movement from ignorance towards understanding as a journey up from darkness into the light:

---

S. Steel (✉)
Calgary Board of Education, Calgary, AB, Canada

A. Homeniuk
Waterford, ON, Canada

© The Author(s) 2019
S. Steel and A. Homeniuk (eds.),
*Suffering and the Intelligence of Love in the Teaching Life*,
https://doi.org/10.1007/978-3-030-05958-3_2

> Like felons used to the darkness, who come up to the light when freed from the depths of some gloomy tower, many trained in common philosophy, and others, will be clutched by fear, seized with astonishment and … thoroughly unsettled.[2]

This manner of speaking about suffering is perhaps most familiar to us. Here, we experience darkness as a bane and light as a balm—albeit one that might expose us to feelings of confusion and perplexity. However, we ought to be aware that the metaphoric portrayal of the soul's illumination as a movement from darkness into light is not the only way to think about the meaning of our suffering. Consider, for instance, a contrary articulation of its meaning, equally profound and equally true, that is offered by the poet Rainer Maria Rilke: "You darkness, of whom I am born / I love you more than all the fires / that fence in the world, / for the fire makes / a circle of light for everyone, / and then no one outside learns of you." Here, darkness is an image for how we experience our Primary Beginning, and our elusively, only-intimated Source. Rilke continues: "But the darkness pulls in everything, / shapes and fires, animals and myself. / How easily it gathers them. / Powers and people / and it is possible a great energy / is moving near me. / I have faith in nights."[3] Observe how wonderfully here Rilke's imagery speaks of the erotic attractions and the sacred pull of mystic night! What undiscovered countries Rilke reveals to us in his preference for night over day—especially when we are ordinarily acclimatized to suppose that only light and the coming into day leads us towards higher truth and understanding. How much deeper we might go in our own quest to understand suffering! Indeed, although we seek out the light in various ways, there is much to be learned from, and sought out, in this darkness.

The compilation you are about to read is designed to entice readers to consider suffering from multiple perspectives in both light and darkness. Fundamentally, this book concerns a forbidden topic for inquiry: *suffering in teaching*. On the one hand, to call it "forbidden" may seem like an exaggeration to many of you who are seasoned teachers; you are only too aware of how common it is for teachers to speak about the difficulties, the injustices, the lack of consideration or appreciation, as well as the trials and abuses they must endure on a daily basis. Indeed, teachers often seem to engage in competitions regarding "who has suffered more" in the profession. At particularly difficult times of the year, such as when we must stay late for Parent Teacher Interviews, when we are swamped with mandatory volunteering obligations, or when we are racing to hit report card deadlines, teacher complaint contests can sound humorously similar to Monty Python's "Four Yorkshiremen" sketch in which the interlocutors try to outdo one another's sufferings, dismissing each other's pains as a "luxury."

But on the other hand, we say it is a *forbidden* subject for inquiry because almost as soon as we began this writing project in early 2016, we were warned *many times* and by diverse people about using the word "suffering" to name our investigations. We were cautioned that uttering this word will make people uncomfortable, and that it will scare them off. It will discourage contributions and confuse people. We were told it "gives off the wrong message." Moreover, we were told that our use of the word "suffering" will turn off publishers, chase away readers, and fatally deplete sales of any book.

Despite these warnings, we affirm that there is great significance and meaning to be found in the consideration of suffering, and in recognizing that all people suffer, *including* teachers. Therefore, whether it is out of a certain stubbornness of spirit, or whether it arises from our steadfastness in the pursuit of truth, we have opted to stay the course in our investigations. After all: simply because inquiry into the subject of *suffering in teaching* is considered taboo or dangerous is no reason to avoid such an investigation. We have stood our ground. And, of course, certain among the prophecies issued to us have come to fruition.

Many of these predictions began to come true almost immediately when an excellent writer, teacher, and wonderful friend of mine who was initially interested in helping to edit the book bowed out. She became disillusioned with the project, partly because thinking about *suffering in teaching* felt so taxing—especially during those short, precious, summer months, when what we *really* want to do most is to relax, to forget, to put-aside, and thereby to *revive* from the grueling nature of our craft as teachers.

Shortly thereafter, many more very fine teachers who we approached, knowing they would be able to share rich perspectives on this subject, declined our invitation and said similar things by way of explanation. Some of them, unsure of their compositional abilities, simply felt unqualified to write; but others who harbored a writer's passion nonetheless were still reluctant to participate; many of them had witnessed much suffering among their own students over the years, and they felt like they themselves had "never really suffered" by comparison. Still others remarked that they couldn't identify with the topic: teaching, in their view, is a "pretty good gig" with "little to complain about."

And yet, it's important for readers to understand that this book isn't a litany of complaints or grievances either.

In the process of compiling the diverse contributions contained in this book, we likewise spoke with a number of our colleagues who had suffered a great deal, but who were not yet finished with their turmoil; still deeply embroiled in facing their own personal storms and torrents, they could not find the distance or peace needed to articulate their experiences, or to lay claim to the grand meaning of the events unfolding before them and within them.

Many more educators who *wanted* to write *could not find the time to write*, for teaching is such a busy and demanding way of life; ironically (given that the Greek word for "leisure" is *schole*, from which we derive our word "school"), the life of a schoolteacher does not easily provide us with the undivided *leisure* in which deep, reflective writing is born and thrives. Writing, after all, involves difficult and uncertain labor mixed with quiet solitude and contemplation. *Writing about teaching in particular* requires a contemplative commitment, and it demands sacrifices from us in other areas of our life. There is a kind of self-inflicted and voluntary suffering in the art of writing. Invariably, writing takes valuable time away from our other duties and interests. *We must carve out a space for the activity of writing*; we must relinquish significant portions of our "down-time" to engage in cloistered, solitary, and quiet contemplation, which naturally means forsaking opportunities to spend time with our precious loved ones and our friends. Writing is, in fact, a kind of self-imposed state of *exile* from the active life and the workaday existence in which we are so deeply immersed as teachers and as servants of the public good. And even having taken pains to carve out such a space, we must then set about the difficult task of *inhabiting* that space, and of cultivating a resilient and daily patience that will allow that space incrementally to affect us through its dark and uncertain processes.

There is love, tenderness, and gestation in the activity of writing. Out of care for their subject, writers must build a kind of nest in which the spirit is prepared to be receptive for the unfolding of what will eventually be written; they must make themselves available for impregnation, outflow, and the overflow that pours forth when the birth pangs of writing finally come. For these and many more reasons, the task of writing about our *teaching-lives* and the meaning we derive from our experiences as educators can be frustrating indeed.

Still others among those we approached were a bit suspicious of the project's core emphasis on *our* suffering as teachers. This focus, they accused, is *unseemly*! Teachers aren't *supposed* to speak about such things, after all: "It's not about *you*: it's all about the children! Put yourself, your ego, and your *own* hurts aside! Serve others. *There* is your transformation." And they have a point.

The teacher's life is one of public service and devotion to the common good. We're supposed to care only about addressing and alleviating the suffering of *others*—namely, our students. Hence, to such people, this book appears to lend itself to navel-gazing and self-indulgent complaining. At the very least, they were concerned that our project might lead to certain *misunderstandings* among the readership regarding teaching. After all, focusing on our pains tends to make those pains bigger. It can easily distort the significance of our discomforts and work *against* the development of insight. Similarly, although teaching is a difficult job, we don't want to make it sound *harder* than it is, or less fulfilling than it is. This group of critics worried that writing a book on such a taboo subject would sound a discouraging note in the profession among its primary audience: teachers and student-teachers.

However, readers should know that this book is intended to inspire, to enthuse, to create solidarity, and to enlighten rather than to discourage them from the teaching-life.

For a number of years, I have from time to time encouraged my high school students to write letters to Patch Adams. Patch is an international teacher of love for one's neighbor. He is a wonderful man, a humble doctor and hospice director; the founder of the *Gesundheit* Institute, a world philanthropist, an itinerant clown, and notably immortalized by Robin Williams in the 1998 film bearing his name. Patch loves to hear from young people. His life is so busy in the service of others all around the world, but he has *always* responded to every letter either my students or I have written to him. When I approached him by snail-mail back in 2016 about the possibility of contributing to this book, Patch responded politely in his cryptic scrawl: "I chose at 18 to never have another bad day as a political act for peace, justice, and care for all people and nature, and have not suffered for 53 years." Then, with a chuckling tone, Patch continued in his letter to me, "If you have food and a friend – what are you bitching about?"

Patch deals with enormous suffering every day in his vital work. He has a deep knowledge of human suffering that informs all his practices, which he tells me are aimed at teaching "love as an intelligence." In much agreement with Patch, we'd like to think that the contents of this book are aligned with that same understanding of teaching.

And yet all of these precautionary notes and reluctances are *not the only challenges* of writing about a topic as provocative as *our own suffering*. Indeed, to a certain extent, Buddhist understanding militates against the writing of such a book. Buddhism embodies one of the longest-standing, greatest spiritual and philosophic traditions of thought, analysis, and writing concerning the nature and the meaning of suffering. When we began this book, I thought *for sure* that it would be relatively easy to find Buddhist writers willing to share their thoughts on our core subject matter.

Not so.

Red flags began to rear up when the Sensei at our local Shinran Buddhist temple here in Calgary very politely informed me that the adage most often attributed to Buddha that "Life is suffering" is actually misleading. He pointed out that the Sanskrit word *dukkha*, here translated as "suffering," actually means something more like "unsatisfactoriness." So if we were to write a book on *dukkha* in teaching, it ought to be called "The *Unsatisfactoriness* of Teaching."

Unfortunately, there is something so… *unsatisfactory* about that title! *Unsatisfactoriness* is such a cerebral-sounding word. Unlike the word "suffering," it doesn't grab you by the guts or speak to your whole being in a visceral way. Moreover, *unsatisfactoriness* doesn't exactly roll off the tongue, nor does it capture one's attention or inspire great interest as a book title. So once again, we pressed forward against all the best advice offered to us about the dangers of our inquiry in the pursuit of knowledge about this elusive, forbidden beast, uncomfortably named *our suffering*.

Similarly, I have a friend with whom I have corresponded over many years. He now lives in China where he teaches English and studies linguistics, but formerly he was the Dharma Master and Head Abbot of the local Avatamsaka Monastery here in Calgary. From time to time, and whenever I am having great difficulties, I seek out his advice and insights. Like his Japanese Buddhist counterpart at the Shinran temple, he too warned me about our pursuit, saying:

> I wouldn't use the word "suffering." Life is suffering according to Buddhists, but most people don't see it that way. It sounds too extreme and fatalistic. I'd use a different word or phrase, perhaps "difficulties" or "trials of teaching," or "the current state of teaching."

Hence, you can see that time-after-time, well-seasoned teachers and devotees to the public good, Senseis and Dharma Masters, *deeply thoughtful people one-and-all*, have counselled us to turn back! However, always having been reckless and renegade in our various ways, Amber and I have never been ones to back down from making a good mistake, or from testing the truths spoken by our betters. So, all-consequences-be-damned, we have opted to maintain the nomenclature of "suffering."

\* \* \*

This book, for better or for worse, concerns suffering in teaching. However, readers should be aware that the term "suffering" need not suggest *weeping* and *wailing* and *gnashing of teeth*. It need not be associated with evil or bad things, pain or complaint, hurt or accusation. Suffering, at its core, has much to do with what Patch Adams called the "intelligence of love."

The ancient Greeks knew this. Their word for suffering was *pathos*. And yet, *pathos* also has the double meaning of *experience*. To suffer is to experience, and to experience is to suffer. Our English words for feeling into the life and the situation of another, *empathy*, or for when we understand and affirm the legitimacy of another person's feelings and situation, *sympathy*, have their deep roots in the awareness that *suffering and experience are one*—as is the love by which we come to know one another informed by *pathos*, suffering, or the deep experience of being.

Unfortunately, nowadays in education there has arisen a great, dominant, and largely unquestioned prejudice *against* the legitimacy of discussing deep, meaningful learning as involving or being rooted in *passivity*. Ever since John Dewey, education revolutionaries and reformers have taken pains to lambast "*passive education*" as intellectually bankrupt, as educationally backward, or destructive. In their view, *passivity* in schools can only be equated with Friere's dreaded "banking model" of education, or the much derided "factory model" of schooling where students are conceived of as *passive* receptacles for the knowledge bequeathed to them by their pedagogical masters.

And yet, the word "passive" is intimately related to *love*, to the experience of being affected by love, and to the illumination provided through having felt oneself claimed by the Lovable. Passivity exists wherever there is openness of mind and spirit, and wherever we find *the intelligence of love*. Our words "passive," "passion," and "passionate" come from Latin roots in *patior, passio,* and *passivus.* These words *all* have to do with suffering, with "the condition of being affected by or acted upon," as well as with strong feeling, emotion, enthusiasm, or *love*.

And of course, we want to have *passionate* students, don't we? Aren't we at our best as teachers when we are *passionate* in our teaching? Speaking religiously or mythologically, we can turn for another example to the *passion* of Christ, which names that short, final period in his life beginning with his arrival in Jerusalem and ending with his crucifixion at Calvary. God's love, and the route to our salvation, is symbolically communicated to us through what befalls his only Son *passively*. Inasmuch as we are like Christ, we too must undergo a kind of passionate conversion through love, which alone enlightens our understanding. These simple images reveal to us that the deepest mysteries of our education are *not* as Dewey and so many others would have them: they are *not active* at their root, but *passive*, just as our own *activity* of loving is itself dependent upon our awareness of the Lovable, or having been affected by the Lovable. This is how self-knowledge and understanding through "the intelligence of love" come to be, after all.

Given our mandate as teachers, so fixated are we upon our students and their well-being, we not-uncommonly forget the ancient command to "Know thyself!" that ought to ground everything we do; consequently, in the mix of things, and in the wear-and-tear of our days, we easily overlook how our ability to serve others has its deepest root in coming to terms with the meaning of suffering in our own lives. Much has been written about students, student suffering, and the responsibilities we bear as teachers toward our students, but perhaps due to the aforementioned prohibition on writing about this topic, very little attention is given to the lives of teachers themselves, and to the role that suffering plays in their professional and personal growth or understanding. This compilation seeks to address that imbalance, particularly because the professional landscape for teachers does not seem to be improving.

★ ★ ★

One of the delightful surprises for *me* in compiling this book was discovering the extent to which *poetry* demonstrated itself to be the primary language in which teachers most poignantly and thoughtfully articulated their deep experiences of suffering and "the intelligence of love." Extra thanks for this insight belongs to Amber Homeniuk, who worked hard to invite poets and artists into our discussions. When we started out three years ago with the idea for this compilation, I had envisioned a book of entirely prose-filled commentaries and reflections. Little did I understand then how difficult and problematic writing about our subject would prove for prospective contributors. Indeed, whether one is a *writer* or a *reader* of this book, the greatest challenge of all with regard to the topic of suffering lies in preparing ourselves for intimate engagement. How does one coax or invite readers towards the openness needed for the investigation of suffering? How does one guide readers to move beyond the most commonly apprehended discomforts or water-cooler discussions of intense or merely irksome experiences in order to deal with what is often uniform, obscured, or subtle, and thereby to spy out what is so readily overlooked? How do we go about helping readers to develop a nuanced ear or a discriminating eye that can see, hear, or otherwise *feel* its way through the coarseness of the suffering which most often presents itself to us? How do we get past the rough, surging flux of events, or the gross aggregate of sensation, thought, and emotion—all those overwhelming, intense experiences and ego-fixations that drag us to and fro from day to day, and from moment to moment? How do we find a calm spot for our own writing to transpire, and how do we persuade our readers to find repose from the torrent of stimulations all around them long enough to listen to their own hearts, and then to dissect and to analyze the constituents of their experiences? In short, how can we prepare our audience for the *receptivity* that is required to develop the "intelligence of love"?

Where prose often fails us, the language of poetry is often more adept at fostering our awareness of and sensitivity for the subtle. Like no other manner of speech, poetry helps human beings to explore nuance, to feel into the elusiveness of being amidst daily situations and events, and to evoke or awaken within us intimations of the ineffable. When we listen to poetry, and when we allow it to attune our sensibilities, poetry can act like an ancient soul-guide or *psychopompos* by leading us down into ourselves in order that we might draw up from those depths "the intelligence of love."

The poems included in this volume have been selected to perform precisely this function. It is hoped that they will prepare and attune the souls of readers for participation in the full range of inquiries regarding suffering in teaching.

\* \* \*

This book is designed for use in Bachelor of Education as well as graduate-level Education courses, but it will most certainly also be of interest to current and diverse servants of the public good, including teachers, instructors, and professors who have long been involved in and committed to the field of education. Each contributor offers readers a unique approach and insightful perspective on suffering and the teaching life with a view to cultivating the "intelligence of love."

This valuable compilation shares insights drawn from suffering by diverse teachers speaking from a variety of points of view. As its editors, we have endeavoured to include contributions from all levels within and outside of the education system in order to ensure broad relevance and connection. By sharing their stories and reflections, our authors hope to shed light upon the dark areas that often are not addressed in Teacher Training Programs, and that generally remain unacknowledged even when we are well-established professionals in the field of education. By speaking about these things, we can help to create a broader sense of community, humanity, and solidarity among teachers.

\* \* \*

*In Light and In Darkness* is divided thematically into six parts in order to highlight provocative linkages and commonalities between the various approaches, concerns, and reflective attitudes displayed among our contributors. Starting with Keith Inman's *Elemental*, which acts as an introduction to the entire corpus of work included in this book, poetry is continuously woven throughout each part as a means to *provoke* as well as to *deepen* reader engagement with central concerns and experiences related to suffering in the teaching life.

The first part concerns the "Analyses of the Meaning of Suffering in Teaching." Beginning with Daniela Elza's poem, *Plato Killed a Moth in My Dream*, readers are initiated into the world of ancient things. In her mystical lines, they will find themselves stirred by flashes of dreams, childhood memories, and by a spirit-which-seeks-understanding; throughout this part, readers are asked to seek out what Elza calls "the True Forms of / our longing." How is *longing* related to the act of educating and being educated? What is at the root of our suffering, and what connection exists between suffering and our longing to know the "True Forms"? Both Sean Steel and Father James V. Schall take up these longings in order to explore questions about the meaning and nature of suffering in relation to the teaching life. Steel examines the classical, three-part distinction concerning the sources of suffering, while also investigating the meaning of suffering in relation to the contemplative awareness of goodness, truth, and beauty. Schall likewise seeks for meaning in the ambiguity of pain and suffering, exploring in particular the significance of courage in the face of evils, and the classical ethical conundrum of whether it is better to do or to suffer injustice.

In the second part, entitled, "Suffering and the Long View: Wisdom Through Experience," we showcase the works of two extraordinary teachers who have devoted their lives to literature, writing, and education. Ontario poet and teacher John B. Lee begins this part of our compilation with, "Oh, my dark companion …" Lee's composition invites readers to engage playfully in a genuine Platonic-anamnetic appreciation wherein "all learning *is* quintessential recall / of the already known." Drawing upon his own deep childhood memories of school, Lee captures insights from the snippets of passing words and deeds. His poetic recollection provides readers with examples of how, in the midst of our own hectic and bustling days, we might, as teachers, "Pursue / *a clear mind and / a loving heart*". Lee's poem is followed by a rumination on the state of teaching by Sandra Ens. A master English teacher herself, Ens weaves thoughtful literary commentary together with candid reflections on the teaching life drawn from years of experience to offer readers a frank portrayal of the state of the profession and the questions we are left with after years of service. We end this part by returning to Lee and his personal essay, "I can't believe it myself most days …" in which he combines a humorous account of his own "defenestration" from the profession with an exposition of the serious and heart-felt teaching experiences of his wife Cathy, and how these vignettes serve as microcosmic events representing larger, troubling trends in education and the manner in which we've come to value one another.

Duly named, "East-Meets-West: Finding Rhythms and Articulating Meaning in Suffering," part three concerns the problems we encounter in seeking to know what *is*, and then in trying to express our intimations and our yearnings for these deepest connections in our quest for self-knowledge. Daniela Elza's writing fosters among readers a receptive awareness for the gaps, spaces, pauses, and for the "quiet temple where the silence gathers / so big it cannot leave the mouth." Beckoning readers to investigate themselves, Elza warns us against supposing that true understanding comes through calculative reason, for what "It thinks it is rational / constantly finds itself *relational*." Musician Harry Manx takes up these themes in his reflection on communication, connection, and the unfurling of insight within his own craft as a consummate blues player who bridges Eastern and Western musical traditions of learning and practice. Manx speaks about the meaning of the blues in relation to suffering, as well as the transformational power of music for creating connection and awakening insights "in a place where thinking gives way to feeling and sensing." We follow Manx's reflection with an excerpt from Tim Ward's classic bestseller, *What the Buddha Never Taught*, in which he records the events of a final meeting with his own teacher, Ajahn Chah. What teachings are to be found in our encounters with suffering? How are such teachings transmitted? These and other questions invite consideration across Eastern and Western perspectives.

In the fourth part of this compilation, we explore "Teaching, Limitations, and Marginalization in Suffering." Artist and writer Kelley Aitken begins our inquiries with some personal observations from her time as an instructor at the Adelaide Resource Centre for Women in Toronto. Aitken's work with women who are suffering in conditions of long-term poverty has demonstrated to her that, for homeless human beings, art can be like "a psychic 'going home,' or 'being at home'." Where all around them, marginalized women meet with ignorance and disregard, artwork says to them: "you exist; this reflects you; your feelings are real." Genuine teaching is, in Aitken's words, "a way to establish intimacy" and "community." Writer, teacher, and activist Dorothy Ellen Palmer offers readers a complementary perspective on community and the suffering brought about through marginalization in her reflection on personal experiences with disability in the classroom. Finally, Red Deer College professor Jenna Butler offers readers some sagely advice on the importance of establishing boundaries and recognizing our personal and professional limitations in the teaching life.

Keith Inman's poem entitled, "Importance" begins our fifth part, "Suffering Spiritual Tensions and the Pursuit of Wisdom in Teaching," with a precious family memory of summertime in which the relentless demands and expectations of the work world are held in tension over against our true delights in learning, where the spirit finds itself happily enraptured by natural wonders and childhood relationality. Inman's poetic articulation of these spiritual tensions is followed by Sean Steel's "A Teacher's Night Song"—essentially a Nietzschean reflection on the manner in which the demands of the teaching profession pose spiritually-corrosive difficulties for those of us who harbour deep yearnings to know the *ground* of things, and who wish to pursue wisdom in our own lives. Daniela Elza's "a shoreline to stand on" presents readers with a distilled poetic expression of the soul's tension-filled searching amidst ambiguity and uncertainty. Following Elza's powerful illumination of the poet-in-search-of-herself, Religious Studies teacher and meditation instructor Stefan Gillow Reynolds offers readers a sensitive, deeply-introspective commentary on his own experiences and struggles with teaching, and in particular with the difficult (if not impossible!) task of living up to the subjects that we teach.

The sixth and final part of our compilation concerns "Suffering, Joy, and Gratitude in Teaching." Here, we begin with Elza's "beauty is embarrassing" in which she plays with an insight drawn from suffering attunement to spiritual tensions, that *"Eros is freedom."* In Elza's work, we see how the poet's quest for self-knowledge bears intimate identity with Patch Adam's "intelligence of love," for both involve knowing "yourself as you are / when you are loved." Next, we hear from political science professor Tom Flanagan. Looking back with gratitude at a wonderful career in post-secondary teaching, Flanagan offers readers an assessment of what might be called the *erotic* nature of education: namely, that awareness we share as teachers and students of our lack, or what Flanagan refers to as a "nagging sense of inadequacy" and a "sort of unfulfilled desire" in education. We follow Flanagan's personal essay with a provocatively-titled piece by Professor Lee Trepanier, "Why Students Don't Suffer." Here, Trepanier is concerned with investigating the structural impediments to developing "interiority," empathy, and sympathy in our institutions of learning. He is keen to understand precisely how certain attitudes and incentives have come to pollute our education system, and served to thwart our students' willingness and ability to suffer—that is, to acknowledge their dependence upon another person and thereby to recognize their own inadequacies. Lee's observational, analytic essay is followed by Kelley Aitken's poem entitled, "The Drawing Lesson", which places readers' consciousness directly amidst the wash of activity, movement, memory, speech, and turbulence in an ordinary art lesson. Reading Aitken's lines of verse, we can feel the excitement and anticipation of classroom activity in tension with the need for calm and focus, where expertise comes into contact with the needs of novitiates; we are made to share in the poet's sense for the challenges of teaching amidst the hurly-burly of expectations with which the teaching life fills us. Moreover, Aitken's poem evokes most poignantly that sense of nostalgia and gratitude that erupts in our own breasts from time to time when, looking back at our interactions with students, we can remember and savour the good that we have done, where "some / vestige of spirit catches", and "Decades later, / whoever looks at these will see her / as we do, tonight." Where Aitken's work would have us recall our interactions with students, Dorothy Warner's chapter, "A Time to Weep and a Time to Laugh, Or, the Necessity of Suffering Even as We Live Happily Ever After" calls upon us to consider the importance of family and the way in which our family experiences have taught us about resiliency in suffering. Finally, we end our compilation with a personal narrative by teacher Christina Alise McDermott, who tells an inspirational story that recognizes and validates certain elements of our suffering and perseverance as servants of the public good.

Amber and I have thoroughly enjoyed bringing all these wonderful authors, artists, professors, teachers, and musicians together in this book project. We are thankful to all of our authors for their candour and excellent contributions, and we hope that you, our readers, find reading *Suffering and the Intelligence of Love in the Teaching Life: In Light and In Darkness* an edifying, inspirational, and vivifying experience.

## Notes

1. Quoted from Aeschylus' *Agamemnon*, lines 179–181. For the original Greek from which Kennedy took his adaptation, see *Aeschylus*, Volume II in Loeb Classical Library. Translated by H. Weir Smyth and H. Lloyd-Jones (Cambridge: Cambridge University Press, 1963).
2. Giordano Bruno, "The First Dialogue," in *Cause, Principle, and Unity*, ed. and trans. Richard J. Blackwell (New York: Cambridge University Press, 1998), 15.
3. Rainer Maria Rilke, *Poems from the Book of Hours* (New York: New Directions Book, 1975).

## REFERENCES

Aeschylus. *Agamemnon*. Volume II in Loeb Classical Library. Translated by H. Weir Smyth and H. Lloyd-Jones. Cambridge: Cambridge University Press, 1963.

Bruno, Giordano. "The First Dialogue." In *Cause, Principle, and Unity*, edited and translated by Richard J. Blackwell. New York: Cambridge University Press, 1998.

Rilke, Rainer Maria. *Poems from the Book of Hours*. New York: New Directions Book, 1975.

PART I

# Analyses of the Meaning of Suffering in Teaching

# Plato killed a moth in my dream

*Daniela Elza*

all night    I chased    moths
around my house.    desperately
waving my arms—    as one *s*inks

behind a pillow.    pawing the air
as another *f*lies high    out of *r*each.
smacking my hands    as a third

(or is it    the same one?)
disappears    in the shadows of my
    rational walls.

my neighbour    Plato    says
he has moths in his  ho*us*e    too.
and he too chases them into his *d*reams

as we yearn toward    the light—

this almost    out of    *r*each

        *at*tempt

---

D. Elza (✉)
Vancouver, BC, Canada
e-mail: daniela@livingcode.org

to grasp         (the True Forms of
                                our longing.

suddenly        I see  a long white moth.
I pick it up.

it sits          on my hand      so white
it gives off     its own light.

does not even         struggle.
I walk to the door.        out to let it go.
meet Plato on my doorstep.        coming in.

holding a moth.        mumbling:
*this one is not*        *the True  moth.*

I look at the Thing  balanced on his palm
and say:        *of course*      *it's not.*
                                *this one's dead.*

then lift my hand to see my moth take *f*light
lighting up     my meta-      physical night.



First published in *the weight of dew* (Mother Tongue Publishing, 2012). Poem reprinted with permission from author.

# Chapter 2: Suffering and the Contemplative Gaze in Teaching

*Sean Steel*

I remember when I first fell in love with school. I was a young boy in grade two, and my teacher was Old Mrs. Haviland. How "old" she was I'm not sure: to us kids, she was *old-as-the-hills*, but in reality, she may have only been around sixty years of age. Old Mrs. Haviland was often called "grouchy" and criticized as "strict" by other students, but to me she was *golden*; where in my previous years I had experienced school as a menacing place of incapacity, constant tears, and almost-daily reprimands, Old Mrs. Haviland was able to wipe all that away with her gaze: with her ability to address *me* in that gaze as a student. That is, each day of class, she looked not just *at* me, but also *into* me. And when she looked inward, she did not see incapacity or a "problem-child"; she found something there worth loving, worth bringing out, and worth cultivating. Her concern to know *me* and to encourage me to know myself made me feel special; it gave me confidence to stretch myself and to hone my abilities as a student. She whetted my appetite for learning and discovery, and ever since that time, I have always felt at home in academic environments where free inquiry and the desire to know reign supreme.

---

S. Steel (✉)
Calgary Board of Education, Calgary, AB, Canada

## Teaching and the Contemplative Gaze

My first experience of the teacher's loving gaze was through Mrs. Haviland all those many years ago. I have since learned that this loving gaze is something that the Greek philosophers referred to as *theoria*, or contemplation. Briefly, *theoria* is the activity of the intellect when it desires "to see" or "to behold" what *is*. The gaze that is *theoria* is not like the desire to master or the lust to dominate that is very often at the heart of our more regular fixation in education with cultivating and demonstrating "critical thinking skills" or "objective knowledge"; the act of *objectifying-in-order-to-know* involves "throwing over against" (in Latin: *ob-iectum*) ourselves that which we seek to know. "Objective knowing" implies separation from what is known, whereas from the contemplative standpoint, we know by loving—that is, we learn through our *union* with what is known, where seer is united with what is seen. Aristotle describes *theoria* or contemplation as the best activity of the highest part of ourselves in relation to its most perfect object. The Greeks spoke of philosophy or "the love of wisdom" as *theoria*, where wisdom or *sophia* is this highest object. Medieval theologians and mystics spoke likewise of *contemplatio*, or that prayerful, solitary activity of the soul seeking after God; similar attitudes towards seeking out knowledge of what *is* have, for millennia, been cultivated through Buddhist Madhyamika philosophy and Hindu Samkhya philosophy, as well as through *vipassana* and *samatha* meditative practices. And although the ultimate end or perfection of these practices might, for instance, be spoken of as the "beatific vision" (*visio beatifica*), as "extinction of self" (*nirvana*), or as the awareness of emptiness (*sunyata*), the significance of *theoria* or contemplation is not restricted to such "culminating" experiences; *theoria* is not as modern authors—and even as a great many ancient critics—have claimed it to be: it is *not* an elitist affair for only the most spiritually-refined and capable adepts. Rather, *theoria* is a quality of existence enjoyed and enjoyable by all human beings even at the level of sensory perception. And certainly it is a mode of existence and a kind of pleasure that is open to and inviting for both teachers and students of all ages. Josef Pieper, a wonderful and insightful Thomistic philosopher who has written extensively about contemplation, sees ample opportunities throughout the day for cultivating a contemplative way of seeing "the things of creation":

A man drinks at last after being extremely thirsty, and, feeling refreshment permeating his body, thinks and says: What a glorious thing is fresh water! Such a man, whether he knows it or not, has already taken a step toward that "seeing of the beloved object" which is contemplation. How splendid is water, a rose, a tree, an apple, a human face – such exclamations can scarcely be spoken without also giving tongue to an assent and affirmation which extends beyond the object praised and touches upon the origin of the universe. Who among us has not suddenly looked into his child's face, in the midst of the toils and troubles of everyday life, and at that moment "seen" that everything which is good, is loved and lovable, loved by God!... Such non-rational, intuitive certainties of the divine base of all that is can be vouchsafed to our gaze even when it is turned toward the most insignificant-looking things, if only it is a gaze inspired by love. That, in the precise sense, is contemplation.[1]

In this beautiful passage, Pieper helps us to understand that contemplation need not be understood as something lofty or unachievable by most people. Rather, bringing our "precise attention" to things in the world as we experience them is itself a form of contemplative "beholding"; as teachers, whenever we direct our attention to what *is*, and inasmuch as we endeavour to help our students do the same, to this same extent might we welcome the contemplative gaze into our own classrooms. And it is precisely here, in this activity of attentive gazing, that education takes on its true and genuine role as the way to our greatest happiness in the pursuit of wisdom.

The "theoretic" or contemplative gaze—that full engagement of the mind and spirit in wondering about and in seeking to know what *is*—is for me what makes school beautiful; it is, moreover, what makes being a teacher the most precious of all occupations. Thomas Aquinas writes that teaching has both an "active" as well as a "contemplative" component. That is to say, teaching, as service to one's neighbour, is rooted in a kind of friendship towards others; we teach out of our desire to share our love of what *is* with our students, and we find tremendous joy in seeing this love of what *is* take hold in their lives as well. This is teaching's "active" component. But precedent to this sharing and nurturing, we must first ourselves love what *is*: we as teachers must attend lovingly to what *is* as seekers of what *is*. This is the "contemplative" component of teaching; sadly, the nature of teaching as a deeply spiritual activity of loving what *is* and of nurturing that love among our students is not generally understood as what defines education. Certainly, teaching is viewed by most administrators and by policy-makers as an enterprise of the "active" life, and they make good and sure of that *in the worst sense*: that is, as teachers, we are worked to the bone and buried alive in expectations without any time at all to engage in the contemplative component of our occupation. We are expected to sacrifice everything "for the children"—our lunch periods, our preparation times, our leisure, our health, our families, even our sanity. Any teacher who suggests for a minute that teaching is not simply the "active" service of one's neighbour—that teaching must *also* involve the cultivation of quiet or solitude, that this might be part of our "professional development," that teaching demands we ourselves continue to cultivate our love for what *is* in the pursuit of wisdom—such a one becomes suspect in the eyes of administrators as "troublesome," "irresponsible," "defiant," "unprofessional," and "not-a-team-player"; such a one is looked on derisively as someone seeking to escape accountability to the processes of school-as-total-work. Such a one is led to suffer even more egregiously.

Indeed, teaching today is mostly held up as a kind of technological process where knowing what *is* has become far less important than knowing how to access information through technological means and showing our students how to do likewise; in all of our confusions about the meaning of learning, and in the allure of fast-paced technological innovations, we tend to lose sight of the fact that *the spiritual basis for teaching is first having seen the truth*! Teaching at its root is necessarily a contemplative activity that involves longing to know what *is*; neither student nor teacher can circumvent the need to contemplate or "to gaze upon" (*theorein*) what *is* (*to on*) by delivery through a technological apparatus. Indeed, technology does not "theorize"; unlike a teacher, it does not *see*, and it does not love the truth, take joy in the truth, or share the truth. On the day that governments hand over teaching to machines as a cost-cutting efficiency (and we are well along this road!), teaching will no longer be teaching; for teaching is, and must remain, a spiritual activity.

## Kinds of Suffering in Teaching

Despite all the madness that infects our thinking about schools, there remains very much to love about teaching. But perhaps to the extent that each of us loves the spiritual activity of teaching, so too in that same measure do we find ourselves liable to greater suffering. Broadly speaking, the contemplative activity necessarily involves a kind of suffering: it requires what Plato refers to in his *Republic* as "suffering the Beautiful." And it is important to stress that this sort of suffering ought not to be eschewed, but rather encouraged among both teachers and students; for when students and teachers are driven by their love or desire (*eros*) to see (*theorein*) the beautiful in all things, their glimpsing of it is itself a kind of suffering (*pathos*) or experience (*pathos*) of what is highest.[2] A truly fruitful educational experience, therefore, implies establishing a kind of wisdom environment in which learners are emboldened, and where they find themselves willing to suffer the hardships of rooting out their ignorance and pretence to knowledge on the one hand, all the while being hearkened to suffer love, the experience of lack or deficiency, and the pain of gazing upon the Lovable on the other hand.

But if teaching as a spiritual activity necessarily involves suffering the Beautiful, so too does it involve less savoury types of suffering; that is to say, teachers, like everyone else, must suffer evil. The Jewish philosopher Moses Maimonides writes that there are three sorts of evil.[3] First, there are those basic evils that we suffer as given to our existence—like sickness, injuries, old age, and loss at the throes of Fortune, for instance. Second, there are those evils that are wrought upon us by others who, either on purpose or unwittingly, do injustice towards us. This sort of evil is greater, Maimonides remarks, than those natural evils that are just given to living. However, by far and above the greatest amount of suffering is *not* caused by natural things, nor is it caused by others who would harm us; rather, it occurs at our own hands, and as a result of our own ignorance.

## On Systemic Suffering and Injustice at the Hands of Others

In a reflection on suffering in teaching, my natural inclination is perhaps to blame others, and to focus upon how school structures add to our suffering as teachers and students: how, for instance, our educational obsessions with the demonstration of knowledge and "thinking skills" in order to earn good grades diverts our attention from what *is*; how the demand that is forced upon teachers by school accountability structures to ensure that their students perform well on high stakes tests and in variegated assessments is itself to blame for much of this confusion and inability to see the true nature of education as the pursuit of wisdom; how the demand—even at the *earliest* ages!—that our students demonstrate what-they-know and *never* what-they-don't-know on pain of failure and punishment creates within them *not* an invitation to wonder, to be amazed, or to appreciate having seen through their own presuppositions to knowledge, but rather instils in them anxiety, fear, rage, and most often rebellion against any educator that would re-direct them towards becoming aware of their ignorance. My tendency, when thinking about suffering, is to speak about my own experiences of how damaging and destructive these social and systemic attitudes towards *not-knowing* and *being-accountable-to-know* are in schools. Indeed, to a certain extent, it is this kind of suffering that, at a certain moment in my life, drove me with great sadness away from teaching, to leave a job that I have loved deeply, and one at which I myself have excelled.

Although I have had a broad range of secondary and post-secondary teaching experiences, my suffering as a teacher from evils of this sort is best illustrated by the contrasts I have experienced during my time at two different high schools. When I began my teaching career, my first school was not what many would call a "high performance" institution. That is to say, it never fared well in provincial rankings based on student achievement test scores. Its teachers, students, and parents were not constantly on edge about marks and grades and success and being-the-best. For instance, I used to post marks by student number at the back of the classroom for my students to peruse; once in a while, students might get up to look at them, but really, marks were of little concern to them; and mostly, parents were just happy that their children were receiving an education, that teachers were working hard each and every day with their sons and daughters, and that their children were taking some amount of pleasure in coming to class. I *loved* teaching at this school. Most refreshingly, I found that many of the students there were interested in exploring questions for their own sake, in thinking about things that they had never before considered, or perhaps things they *had* tried to think about on their own, but had never found a competent guide to assist them in their musings. During my years at this school, I developed many wonderful relationships with my students. *Here* was a school where Old Mrs. Haviland's contemplative gaze might find a welcoming home, and all these years later, I find myself still in contact with many of my students from that time. Even now, on the odd chance of meeting with any of them, or when discussing with them through email or social networks,

I am always brought great pleasure in the experience of that deep and lasting mutual bond.

My second high school was quite different in character, and my experience of teaching there was entirely opposite in tone. Where my first school had been "mediocre" by all standard academic accountability measures, this second school was *always* near the top of the provincial rankings. Affluent parents yearned to have their children sent there; teachers and administrators patted themselves on the back for the high levels of achievement their pedagogy seemed to effect on the student populace. Concerns about always-being-at-the-top were further enforced by the school's measures to "cream" the students into "honours" and "advanced placement" (AP) classes—ostensibly with the goal of improving, "diversifying," and "enriching" student learning, but more likely because such programs were demanded by those who desired to feel pride in being part of an elite group recognized for its higher grades—for its pretensions to know and to be able to demonstrate masterful knowledge. At my previous school, my manner of teaching through guided readings from "the great texts," dialogic questioning, inducing perplexity, and friendly regard to share my love of what *is* with my students bore beautiful fruit; however at this second school with its hypertrophied fixation on academic achievement, it seemed as though all my efforts were in vain. The loving gaze upon what *is* rarely—if ever—caught hold in any of my charges; as in the Zen koan, students were so entirely focused upon *the finger* of grades that they were, by and large, unable to recognize its reference to *the Moon*. Every single PD was focussed on how to measure and to assess students ever more accurately, and how to improve student *grades*. Moreover, parents hot for success and acclaim as the only hope for their children's happiness blamed any pedagogy that was *not* aimed directly at accomplishing these things; leading students in discussions and questions that ended in perplexity, in confusion, or in wonder about deeply unanswerable things struck many of them as suspiciously irresponsible if not incompetent pedagogy: it certainly was *not* "teaching my son (or daughter) how to write an essay for the achievement tests!" Students, too, were acclimatized at this school to demand certainty in knowledge; they didn't want questions; they wanted answers! After all, such certainty is what is needed in order to gain entrance into law school, into med school, into astronaut school, or whatever. In short, where at my previous school I had felt at home, deeply connected with many of my students in a mutual quest for what *is*, and able to encourage among them the loving gaze that is contemplation, at this school I felt alone and alienated in my search, unconnected and unable to connect with my students, with parents, with administrators, and even with most of my fellow teachers. I felt not like a teacher at all, but rather more like a waiter at a table whose job was only to serve up whatever squalid food was being demanded by the appetites and ambitions of my customers and my boss. This is the nature of the second sort of suffering pinpointed by Maimonides as it pertains to teaching; for it is this sort of suffering that arises according to the injustices of the educational system and that erupts either voluntarily or unwittingly from the actions of others: it is the suffering of the teacher who finds himself or herself unable to teach when inquiry into the contemplative ground of teaching is prohibited (on pain of wrath and endless quarrelling) by the structures and demands of his or her profession. I have, moreover, found this stark contrast consistently replicates itself at the post-secondary level in B.Ed. Programs as well.

## On Self-Inflicted Suffering That Stems from Ignorance

Although it may be my natural inclination to focus on suffering that arises from the second type of evil, following Maimonides' insights it is more honest to say that the lion's share of my suffering as a teacher has arisen from the third form, *at my own hands*, and as a result of my own ignorance. The teacher, like his or her students as well as the rest of humanity, is beset by internal disorders, much in the way of pride and fear, sadness and disappointment, anger and resentment, arrogance and desire, and *much* pretence to knowing. In my experience, the very best way to respond to this third form of suffering is to direct one's own pedagogy at it, not only for our own benefit as teachers, but for the benefit of our students as well. As an English teacher, I have been doubly-blessed in this regard, for the teacher-of-literature has an opportunity like no other to engage in what the Buddhists call *upaya*, or "skilful means" that might liberate sentient beings from suffering. Where the typical attitude towards literary study in the classroom is to use literature as a means to assess and to develop student critical thinking across Bloom's taxonomy of learning, the skilful practitioner subverts this process by *simultaneously* drawing learning in the classroom towards its contemplative function.

Just as much of what causes the teacher to suffer is the result of internal disorders of the soul with regard to appetites, desires, fears, and so forth, so too is much of the difficulty that our students face with learning related to similar internal dysfunctions and their own lack of psychic order. In my grade 10 English classes, for instance, I have often enjoined students to participate in guided readings of Shakespeare's *Julius Caesar* as well as selections from the autobiographical works of Mohandas Gandhi. Both authors offer us excellent examples of figures who engage themselves and others in the quest for internal harmony and psychic order as the true source for social or societal order. In *Julius Caesar*, Brutus the Stoic stands out as "the best of the Romans" precisely because of his mind's rule over his lower, passionate self. Brutus' example is instructive *for students* in the average adolescent classroom, where self-control and mindfulness are in short supply. However, Brutus' example is especially instructive *for teachers* due to its deficiencies; for Brutus' inability to secure Rome from tyranny and his consequent grizzly death arise from nothing else but his own failure to extend his contemplative gaze outward; that is, although he recognizes the true order of the soul and makes this ordering his *own* foundation, he fails to see or to address the state of soul prevalent among his countrymen. *He does not see them*; rather tragically, *he supposes that they are all like him*—that they have all remained or aspire to be "true Romans" as lovers of republican virtues and freedom, when in fact, the Romans around him have debased themselves in their thirst for pleasures and comforts. In terms of thinking about our own suffering, the contemplative-teacher must be wary of Brutus' fate; as teachers, we must approach leadership in our classrooms with Shakespeare's contemplative insight and warning in mind: namely, that students are by and large like the Roman plebes; in fact, the same goes for administrators, parents, and other faculty, actually; they *do not* generally seek out the freedom of the spirit that is afforded by theoretic gazing, and given the choice, they will most often take the comforting or familiar path over the one that asks of them greater spiritual discipline, heightened uncertainty, extended commitment—and all this for invisible and intangible ends! Hence, in order to lead students successfully as a contemplative-teacher, one must ensure, to the best of one's abilities, that one has seen into the psychological make-up of one's audience—that one knows to whom one is speaking; moreover, such a one must take the greatest care to secure his or her own classroom from the Antonys of the world—from those caustic and demagogical forces external to real learning that might destroy any education aimed at the pursuit of wisdom. This is the great challenge of teaching to end the third sort of suffering in the classroom, just as it is the great challenge of politics in *Julius Caesar*.

Gandhi's example of the practice of *satyagraha* offers both students and teachers a valuable opportunity for meditative seeing (*theoria*) aimed at a clearer vision of (and therefore union with) the lovable. *Satyagraha* is literally firmness (*agraha*) in Truth (*satya*); put another way, it is the steadfast love of what truly *is*. Gandhi refers to it throughout his writings as "soul-force." In order to develop such firmness in Truth or "soul-force," Gandhi contends that each of us must exert efforts to cultivate the cessation of all our earthly desires, of all those passions and thoughts that drive our everyday actions, and that constitute the source of all our suffering. Speaking of this chastity-of-spirit (*brahmacharya*), Gandhi writes: "To attain to perfect purity one has to become absolutely passion-free in thought, speech and action; to rise above the opposing currents of love and hatred, attachment and repulsion." Essentially, in order to practice *satyagraha*, "I must reduce myself to zero."[4]

This statement always shocks students, who are used to and demand an education designed *not* to reduce but to engorge the self with its ambitions, its dreams, and its thirsts for success and notoriety. Moreover, education systems "for the Twenty-First Century" are increasingly concerned with amplifying our technological fixations, with tailoring every educational minute in the classroom to the psycho-mental identity of each student, and with personalizing and individualizing curriculum and curriculum delivery; indeed, much of the allure of so-called "educational technology" seems to lie in its power to offer the individual "I" increased power or control over its environment; in particular, these technologies provide users with variegated abilities to shape their interactions within that environment to their own personal preferences—hence the mad rush at the malls to purchase the latest connection to the "i" in our iPhones, our iPads, and our iPods. In short, the arc of our educational efforts runs exactly counter to the contemplative requirements of *brahmacharya* for the cultivation of "soul-force."

During Gandhi's time, it was not unusual for thousands of Hindus to flock towards him in pilgrimage in order that they might "gaze upon" or take *darsana* from him; that is, by *seeing* Gandhi, Hindu pilgrims saw some glimmer of the Truth of what *is*. Similarly in our own classrooms, by *seeing* Gandhi—that is, by being challenged to wrestle with the truth of his words through carefully guided discussions—our students may likewise be made pilgrims for Truth engaged in contemplative *seeing*, in *darsana*, or *theoria*. They may, perhaps, have their love of Truth whetted and their attachments to the psycho-mental "i-" questioned. They may, in this fashion, be led into the orbit of a genuine education directed at their highest happiness in the pursuit of wisdom. And so too may the teacher who reads Gandhi's words alongside his or her students be reminded of the real meaning of education, thereby lessening some of his or her own suffering amidst the turmoil of the classroom and its constant tendencies towards deterioration and the loss of sight of what *is*. Moreover, Gandhi's writings have a special teaching just for teachers!—a revelation that overcomes the deficiencies already noted in Brutus' example. Briefly, where Brutus sought to restore freedom to the Roman Republic *without* recognizing or seeing into the true nature of his countrymen, Gandhi's quest for "home rule" (*Hind Swaraj*) was not fraught with similar delusions. In his discussion of *Hind Swaraj*, Gandhi admits that he knows "India is not ripe for it":

> The only part of the programme [that is, the practice of *satyagraha* in order to attain home rule] which is now being carried out is that of non-violence. But I regret to have to confess that even that is not being carried out in the spirit of the book. If it were, India would establish Swaraj in a day. If India adopted the doctrine of love as an active part of her religion and introduced it in her politics, Swaraj would descend upon India from heaven. But I am painfully aware that that event is far off as yet.[5]

Just as Gandhi saw that the only real peace and the only true rule must come from within ourselves as an emanation of the proper ordering of the soul in relation to Truth, so too must the contemplative-teacher recognize that true peace and order in the classroom cannot be brought about by that sort of education that is most sought after by teachers, parents, administrators, policy-makers, and students: the education-for-success will *not* alleviate suffering of the third sort. Only by example, only by embodying the attitudes of *brahmacharya* and *satyagraha* and by becoming oneself an example from which one's own students can take *darsana* might the teacher alleviate not only his or her own suffering, but the suffering of others as well.

## Concluding Remarks: The Conundrum of Suffering and the Contemplative Gaze

My own experiences and practices as a teacher have led me to discover a kind of conundrum that arises from the problem of suffering in teaching. On the one hand, it seems to be the case that we can only counteract suffering that arises from the third sort of evil through incorporating contemplative practices into our pedagogy. Indeed, because teaching itself is necessarily both "active" and "contemplative," we can only truly be teaching if we ourselves engage in contemplation or *theoria*. However, on the other hand, by doing so we invite *additional* suffering into our classrooms, for we suffer the wrath of students, parents, and administrators who demand an-education-for-success rather than an-education-for-wisdom; and our students suffer likewise because of their conditioning according to systemic and societally-reinforced assumptions about education which portray not-knowing and the realization of one's ignorance not as a blessing but rather a curse and a harbinger of doom.

Nevertheless, although our efforts as contemplative-teachers to alleviate suffering of the third kind are bound to bring suffering of the second kind down upon our heads and the heads of our students, *we must in good conscience continue to do so*. For as Maimonides points out, the second form of suffering is of lesser consequence and is far less ubiquitous than the third which is, after all, responsible for the lion's share of our suffering. And indeed, it may be that part of our development as teachers (and of course as human beings) involves the cultivation of the virtues of courage and temperance. That is, when we practice teaching contemplatively, when we cultivate mindfulness and enjoin our students to participate in "the loving gaze," we must, at the same time, bravely face the second sort of evil that is directed towards us from all corners; nor must we intemperately succumb to our desires for pleasure or comfort by taking the easier route which might win us more praise from parents and students; indeed, it has been my honest experience as a teacher that—although it may *feel* like it—really, it is *not* the case that the greatest hardships and sufferings arise for contemplative-teachers at the hands of others who fail to understand and who denigrate the genuine calling of the teacher; although it may most tangibly appear to us that the contemplative component of teaching is indeed under continual attack and subject to the harshest ridicule by deeply ignorant people, it is not possible for anyone who might wish to do us harm to prohibit us from doing what is best: rather, what will in the end thwart us is only our own cowardice in the face of their threats and in facing our own fears; or again, it may be our own lack of temperance in regards to the attractions of pleasure and accolades that swell our pride that make us most likely to leave off from the contemplative life that necessarily undergirds all true teaching. In short, *we*, and *not others*, are to blame for most of our suffering, just as Maimonides teaches us. And if we are resilient in our attention to the third sort of suffering, we may find in the end that even the second form will lessen its grip upon us and those in our charge; for by dedicating ourselves to the activity of unearthing our own ignorance as well as the ignorance of our students, and by seeking out wisdom in an ever-more perfect vision of what *is*, perhaps we might incrementally shape or change the societal attitudes and systemic structures that give rise to the second form of suffering which always dogs contemplative practitioners at the hands of the purely active ones.

## NOTES

1. Josef Pieper, *Happiness and Contemplation*, trans. Richard and Clara Winston (South Bend: St. Augustine's Press, 1998), 84–85.
2. The suffering involved in "turning around" (*periagein*, 515c) to seeing the beautiful is most famously depicted in Plato's *Republic*, particularly in the image of the ascent from the cave's darkness into the light of the sun, during which the eyes are pained and momentarily blinded by the sun's brilliance (515c–516b). See Plato, *The Collected Dialogues*, eds. Edith Hamilton and Huntington Cairns, Bollingen Series 71 (Princeton: Princeton University Press, 1961).
3. Moses Maimonides, *The Guide for the Perplexed*, trans. M. Friedlander (New York: Dover Publications, 1956), III.xii.
4. Mohandas Gandhi, *An Autobiography: The Story of My Experiments with Truth*, trans. M. Desai (Boston: Beacon Press, 1993), Chapter 168.
5. Mohandas Gandhi, "A Word of Explanation," in *Hind Swaraj* (Delhi: Rajpal & Sons, 2010), 12.

## References

Gandhi, Mohandas. *An Autobiography: The Story of My Experiments with Truth.* Trans. M. Desai. Boston: Beacon Press, 1993.
Gandhi, Mohandas. *Hind Swaraj.* Delhi: Rajpal & Sons, 2010.
Maimonides, Moses. *The Guide for the Perplexed.* Trans. M. Friedlander. New York: Dover Publications, 1956.
Pieper, Josef. *Happiness and Contemplation.* Trans. Richard and Clara Winston. South Bend: St. Augustine's Press, 1998.
Plato. *The Collected Dialogues.* Ed. Edith Hamilton and Huntington Cairns. Bollingen Series 71. Princeton: Princeton University Press, 1961.

# Chapter 3: On the Two Meanings of Suffering

## James V. Schall

The following chapter takes readers on a far-reaching excursion into the meanings and purposes of suffering. This essay begins by discussing some important distinctions between suffering and evil, as well as between pain and injustice. It then draws readers' attention to the manner in which our learning is contingent upon our being affected by (or suffering) the world of events around us. By reflecting upon our nature as "beings who undergo and suffer many things," this essay highlights the value of our suffering in relation to the cultivation of compassion, understanding, and courage. Finally, the author book-ends his reflection on suffering with a thoughtful analysis of the ancient Socratic dictum that "it is better to suffer evil than to do it." Let us begin with quotations from Plato and Leo the Great. The content of these quotations informs all the analysis that follows:

> *Polus*: 'Surely the one who's put to death unjustly is the one who's both to be pitied and miserable.' *Socrates*: 'Less than the one putting him to death, Polus, and less than the one who's justly put to death.' *Polus*: 'How

---

J. V. Schall (✉)
Los Gatos, CA, USA
e-mail: James.Schall@georgetown.edu

© The Author(s) 2019
S. Steel and A. Homeniuk (eds.),
*Suffering and the Intelligence of Love in the Teaching Life*,
https://doi.org/10.1007/978-3-030-05958-3_5

can this be, Socrates?' *Socrates*: 'It's because doing what's unjust is actually the worst thing there is.' *Polus*: 'Really? Is that the worst? Isn't suffering what is unjust still worse?' *Socrates*: 'No, not in the least.'"[1]

To pay the debt of our sinful nature, a nature that is incapable of suffering was joined to one that could suffer."[2]

# I

Leo the Great's remarks imply that the reality of suffering is almost inevitably associated with the notion that it ought not to be. Even though suffering now exists, it seems that God should have simply removed it rather than Himself somehow suffering its results. Isn't suffering a blot on existence itself? Suffering seemed related to evil. Many even (wrongly) identify suffering with evil. Leo also implied, however, that the divine had to deal with evil once it did exist through the free choices of men and angels. The divine plan for dealing with evil was accomplished, unexpectedly, through Christ suffering its consequences in His own person.

Thus, in this light, do we consider suffering itself to be an evil, nothing more, nothing less? But suffering itself is not exactly the same as evil. It is something that somehow ought not to exist but does. When we begin to think of suffering, however, we find ourselves taking a more careful look at it. "Is suffering really an evil as such?" we ask ourselves. Or is it a consequence of some evil? What would our world be like if it had no suffering within it? Could it even exist without it?

In the very beginning of our literature, we find in Sophocles the affirmation that "Man learns by suffering." Here suffering is not presented as something entirely negative. We wonder if there are things we could not learn except by suffering. Needless to say, every person in his lifetime will have to deal with suffering, either his own or that of others, either great or small. Part of being a human is simply, once we encounter it, to think about what suffering means in our own life and in the lives of others. How we respond to the suffering of others tells us much about who we are. How we deal with our own suffering reveals as much as anything else the truth about our character.

Every day almost, we come across random pieces of advice about suffering. Advertisements about "pain relievers" are a staple of commercial television, newspaper, and magazine advertising. Dentistry has become largely painless. Even our dying is accompanied by medications that lessen any pain. Paul admonishes us in Romans (12:12): "Be patient in sufferings." Evidently, something is wrong with being overly "impatient" in suffering. We have all met people who have little place for suffering in their lives, who make scarce attempt to face its reality. They become demanding and blame others for their condition.

Some more utopian thinkers talk about a "right" not to suffer. Indeed, "suffering" is given as an excuse for euthanasia of ourselves or others. Suffering is said to have no purpose. The assumption with Paul's admonition, however, is that we have, or ought to have, some control over our sufferings or at least our reaction to them. To suffer patiently implies that suffering may have a purpose. It does not exist in the universe or in our lives for no reason. Modern medicine is devoted to the control of pain and suffering. It has made many welcome advances in reducing it, though other forms of suffering keep occurring.

Intrinsic to Christianity is the notion of "vicarious suffering". That is, the patient suffering of someone else can supply what is lacking in us. And vicarious suffering leads to the question of the suffering of the innocent, or even of the animals, issues that have perplexed mankind from its origins almost. We also encounter a difference between spiritual and physical suffering. A toothache is one thing; the grief over a sick child is another. We usually reserve the word "pain" for physical suffering, though it can also serve for spiritual suffering. These considerations provoke us to sort out the place of "suffering" in our lives and in our world. We do find a few philosophies that want to deny that pain exists; that it is an illusion. But this is not a majority opinion. And it is also true that some people are more sensitive to pain than others. What is immediately clear is that we cannot suffer someone else's pain.

The word "compassion", to be sure, means to suffer with someone else. There is an old saying to the effect—"save me from a doctor who has never suffered himself." When we have a broken leg, or cancer, or pneumonia, it is always good to meet someone else who has had these issues. Not only can they tell us something of what to expect, but they can understand better what we are going through. They can see the limits of what to expect of someone in our condition. But the fact that someone else has had a broken leg does not change the experience we are going through. We still must go through it ourselves. Compassion, if we are not careful, especially in spiritual and moral matters, can lead us to excuse the cause of those sufferings in our own chosen disorders. The suffering then becomes an excuse for not facing the real cause of the problem.

## II

As we have intimated in the title of these considerations, the word "sufferings" can have two broad meanings. It can mean pain of various sorts, physical or mental. But "to suffer" something also can mean undergoing something whether from natural or voluntary causes. When Christ, in a famous English translation, said, "Suffer, little children, to come to me",[3] He was not talking about how annoying it is sometimes to deal with little children. Quite the opposite, He wanted to let them come to Him as something delightful and good (Matthew 19:14). Much of our existence concerns not what we do to others, but what happens to us whether we like it or not. We are beings who undergo or suffer many things to happen to them.

If it rains on us, for example, we are not exactly "suffering" unless it is chilly and we have no umbrella or raincoat. We are "suffering" the rain to fall on us. It is just coming down as it is supposed to and we are caught in it. As the musical "Singing in the Rain" showed, it may in fact be quite pleasant to have it rain on us, to let it rain on us, to delight in rain. After all, we "suffer" in another sense when it does not ever rain. We can say, even though it has no power of choice, that the ground "lets" or "suffers" the rain to fall on it. We also say that the ground "suffers" when it does not rain in a drought, though I suppose it does not make any difference to the dirt itself one way or another. We are the ones who need the rain for our purposes.

First, let us take the understanding of "suffering" as what happens to us. We are beings for whom many things must happen outside of our control without which we cannot exist. The whole of our existence is predicated on the fact that the cosmos itself exists. Within that cosmos, sun, moon, our planet, the laws of motion and gravity already are in place. The earth itself has been about for some four billion years. Most of the things we need to survive were provided before human beings appeared on the planet. When human beings did appear, they had to "suffer" many things that, in turn, incited them to learn how to cope with them. So there seems to be some correlation between what was here and our learning how to make it work for our needs. Presumably if man never suffered from cold or heat, starvation or sickness, he would never have needed to figure out ways to deal with any one of them. There was a relation between what the earth could provide and man's gradual learning how better to provide it.

Man did not "develop" himself so that he had a mind that could deal with what was not himself. His mind was already an essential element in what he was. He did not "make" it but he did need to learn to use it. His mind by itself could "do" nothing but know things. This power to know was no mean power. However, it was clear that he was connected to the world also by his hands, not just through his mind. Indeed, the coordination between his mind and his hands seemed to be part of the designation of what he was. Thus, when something "happened" to him, when he "suffered" some movement from the skies or the fields or from other human beings that involved him, he would first have to figure out what it was. He would have to learn what to do about it. Finally, he would make something that would mitigate or improve what happened. This development is really the story of civilization. And we should not forget that what was once learned can be forgotten unless we preserve it.

So it is not so bad after all that we have to "suffer" some things, things that just, to our surprise, happen to us. Without them, we would not have made any effort to confront them. In a way, things, in their turn, have to "suffer" us, our power and capacity to "do" things or "make" things. We are agents of change and of preservation. We are, in short, beings to whom things happen. We might wonder why everything was not given to us in the first place. But that would mean that we would have to do nothing either but "suffer" or receive things with no input of our own.

So all the vast energy and confusion that resulted in our not knowing everything from the beginning, everything we had to "suffer" being done to us, turned out to give us something that we could not have had in any other way. We do not just "want" the things we need or make us happy. We also want some input into their coming to be so that we learn something from what we "suffer". Thus, far from it being a bad or evil thing that God did not provide everything for us; it is closer to a blessing as it was the occasion for us to be more fully what we see ourselves to be when we have figured things out. Such things, to be sure, were somehow there to be figured out. And our capacity to do the "figuring out" was also something initially given to us as a central capacity of what we are.

## III

Let us take a look at suffering when it means pain. With some reflection, we can see that the fact that we have a body that can suffer pain is a good thing. This is the kind of being we are. We are especially aware of our bodily-ness when we are sick. The first thing that the nurse or doctor wants to know, on examining us, is: "Where does it hurt?" Clearly, if we have a tightness in the heart or an ache the ear, we ought not to say that the pain is in the "foot" or "stomach". And even when we describe as accurately as possible where the pain is located, we may still need more sophisticated instruments—X-Rays or MRIs—to find out its exact location in our bodies. But suppose that we did not have any "pain" that went along with some physical disorder. Then we would not be warned by pain somewhere in our bodies that something was wrong. However painful a toothache or a heart seizure may be, it is clearly a good thing that pain tells us something is wrong. And the more intense it is, the more urgent it is to do something about it. We assume that pain will tell someone, the doctor at least, what is wrong. Hopefully, the profession will have learned something about alleviating such a problem.

In this sense, then, pain is quite a good and necessary thing for our overall well-being. It goes along with the "design" of what we are. It is a messenger; it is not itself the problem but an indication that a problem exists. What is in fact more remarkable is that normally things go well; we do not think of pain because we do not suffer anything. None of us want to suffer pain, but neither do we want not to suffer when something is wrong. Otherwise, our lives would be much shorter and more painful than they are. When we think about it from this angle, suffering becomes more intelligible. We can see that pain has a natural purpose.

Indeed, the very notion of courage was related to this issue of pain and suffering. The virtue of courage was rightly considered the first and most basic of the virtues. It was the virtue aimed at keeping us alive before the dangers and sufferings that accosted us. The object of courage, that which it was designed to control, was precisely our felt pains and hurts. Courage was directed at our response to the actual sufferings and pains that happened to us either in war, or in health, or in protecting ourselves or in other forms injustice. The habit of courage meant that we were prepared to endure a certain amount of suffering and pain so that we might do what we ought in other areas.

Courage, thus, was a good habit. Its corresponding vices, one too much and one too little, were rashness when we showed no understanding of the extent of the dangers, or cowardice when we failed to do the basic things needed to protect our lives or goods or those of others for whom we were responsible. Courage was acquired by doing courageous acts. It was not enough just to know what it is. We had to form ourselves, both to understand what it is and to do it in fact when the occasion arose. A definition of courage, a knowledge of what it meant, needed to be in our head. We were to understand what we were doing. We also needed actually to be courageous when occasion arouse. A courageous person, thus, was a person who was able to overcome his fears or pains so that he could do what needed to be done.

Many are the things that, in the course of our lives, we may need to do that will cause pain ranging from giving birth to children, to being wounded in accidents or wars, to standing for the truth when called upon. We will have to face pain and, as the testimony of others teaches us, we can do so but only if we rule ourselves to do so. If some overwhelming pain or suffering comes that no one could possibly resist, say we are caught in an earthquake, then we must suffer the consequences. The world recognizes the importance of courage. Without it, no family, or school, or country, or institution could last.

## IV

No doubt the most famous and, in many ways, the most important principle that we encounter in thinking of suffering is that which comes, as we saw in the beginning citation, from Socrates. In its briefest form, it tells us: "It is better to suffer evil than to do it." To understand why this principle is true is perhaps the chief contribution political philosophy can make to civilized life which depends on its validity to stand. Many thinkers have wanted to define freedom as the "power" to do whatever we wanted, whatever it was, even evil. It was claimed to be wrong to "suffer" anything. It revealed weakness. The greatest evil was thus to "suffer" death when we could escape it by lying or killing the innocent. In this sense, courage was exalted to mean doing anything we wanted with no restrictions of truth or justice to hamper us.

Why was this view wrong? Civilization is built on the principle that "It is never right to do wrong; hence, it is better to suffer evil than to do it." If we authorize or encourage people, especially political leader or professors, to do what is evil as a part of the tools of their profession, we have no longer any grounds to object when they do whatever they want to us. We can only appeal to greater power, if there is any. We cannot appeal to what is true and just.

But the fact is that many people, including Socrates himself, have been confronted with this alternative: Either do what is evil or die. This issue is the one that most famously brings us to the heart of courage.

Briefly, the ultimate test of the courageous man is not his ability to save his life no matter what threatens him, but his willingness to prefer death to doing what is evil. This test is true both in private lives and, more famously, in public life. The unjust state will always claim the power to eliminate not just those who commit crimes, but those who object to its policies, especially those policies that take innocent lives.

Socrates had also said that nothing evil can happen to a good man. This position brought him to the famous question of whether death itself was an "evil", since many a good man, including Socrates himself, not to mention Christ, suffered death at the hands of the state in a formal trial. Indeed, the question was, in the formulation of Hobbes, whether death was the worst evil. If it was, as Hobbes, contrary to Socrates, thought it was, then someone could make us do whatever he wanted simply by threatening or carrying out death against us. In that case, our death had nothing to do with right or wrong, only with our not having sufficient power to protect ourselves. No one doubted that death was an evil in some sense, even though it came to every man in one way or another. So this famous question of whether it is better to suffer evil than to do it brings us to the basic question of whether the preservation of human life itself, which is undoubtedly a good thing, is the only consideration needed when death is threatened.

Thus, if we look at the phraseology of the proposition, we see that the issue is over "suffering" death or "doing" evil. What is the difference? The virtue of courage is usually seen as overcoming obstacles of war, hunger, or endurance that would ensue if we did not suffer finally to gain what is needed to stay alive and protect others. But obviously, there are times when this endeavor fails. Death is the only alternative open. We look at the issue from the side of the one who has such an alternative presented to him. That is, suffer death or commit some mandated evil, whatever it is. If we stay alive but sacrifice all other goods, this defines our soul forever. Death is, for us, the greatest evil, contrary to Socrates' principle.

This view that death is not the worst evil is based on the fact that an objective order of things exists. Everyone, including the one threatening death, is bound by the rule not to do evil. In Socrates' and Christ's cases, the "trial" that reached the decision to kill them was, at best, legally in order. It thus fell into the category of an unjust ruling on the part of those who carried it out. It was contrary to what was indeed the proper law in nature.

The one who was killed did not morally participate in the killing. He "suffered" an evil to happen to him. This understanding is basic for it means that the person killed stood for a principle that he upheld and testified to by his death. The ones making and carrying out the sentence violated the rule of justice and reason. The next issue followed immediately. The unjust man violated the law with impunity, whereas the just man was killed.

This situation left the perplexing question: "Is the world itself then created in injustice if injustice prevailed in it?" It was to this situation that Socrates proposed the immortality of the soul and the judgment of each person according to his deeds after death. However it might seem in this world, injustice does not go unpunished. The rule of reason will be upheld. In the end, the ones who did evil did receive the greatest of punishments. Those who suffered evil received the highest rewards. In this sense, the virtue of courage upholds what is right. No evil did come to the just man even in his death. Death is not the worst evil. The worst evil is to do what is wrong and not to repent of it.

This point enables us to see the reasons why punishment is connected with injustice. Generally, every norm or law should have a proper punishment connect with its violation and a reward for its observation. These rewards and punishments are consequences of observing or not observing the law, which should be followed primarily because it is reasonable to do so. The specifics of the law exist, in other words, to uphold justice. Rewards and punishments are but consequences of how we choose to help us do what we ought even if there were no rewards or punishments.

In conclusion, then, the two meanings of suffering take us to the very depths of our reflection on the kind of beings we are. Indeed, to reflect on these things is one of the basic purpose of our education. That is, we should have the opportunity to see these things spelled out for us in our literature and in our philosophy so that we can see what is at stake in our lives. These issues of pain and injustice, of suffering and doing, will certainly come up, in one form or another, in every human life. Not to think about them will not prevent their occurrence.

But thinking alone is not enough, as Aristotle taught about every virtue. We must actually practice being brave to be virtuous and to do so when the occasion arises. We are beings to whom things happen. We are also beings who understand and choose that "It is never right to do wrong." A civilization not built on this principle may stand, but it will stand against what its citizens ought to be. It is the function of our thinking that we need to learn what we ought to be, even when are taught that death is the greatest of evils—which it isn't.

## Notes

1. Plato, "Gorgias," in *Plato: The Collected Dialogues*, ed. Edith Hamilton and Huntington Cairns, Bollingen Series LXXI (Princeton: Princeton University Press, 1961), 469b.
2. Leo the Great, *Breviary*, Second Reading, March 25. See Epistle 28 *ad Flavanium*, 3–4. See www.ebreviary.com.
3. Matthew 19:14.

## References

Leo the Great. *Breviary*. Second Reading, March 25. From Epistle 28 *ad Flavanium*, 3–4. See www.ebreviary.com.

Plato. "Gorgias." In *Plato: The Collected Dialogues*. Ed. Edith Hamilton and Huntington Cairns. Bollingen Series LXXI. Princeton: Princeton University Press, 1961.

*The New Oxford Annotated Bible*. New Revised Standard Version. Ed. Bruce M. Metzger and Roland E. Murphy. New York: Oxford University Press, 1991.

PART II

# Suffering and the Long View: Wisdom Through Experience

# Oh, my dark companion …

*John B. Lee*

my sister tells me the story
of how
when she was a girl
she witnessed the arrival
at the girls' door of SS No 6
the village elementary school
we attended as children
and she and her friends
watched as Miss Myrtle Downie
walked up to unlock the building
as was her morning practice
and there
sheathed over the handle
some local wag
had affixed an unused prophylactic
skinning the knob
like a blister on brass
and she peeled the latex
as an audience giggled shyly behind their hands
placed the safe to her lips

and inflated the thing
as though she were about to amaze them all
with a poodle balloon

and I thought as the tale unfolded
how some rough-living prankster
some nearly-shaving rogue
some going-on-for-sixteen quitter
might have been there
secreted nearby and hiding behind
one of the *pump-pump pole away* maples
those tag-and-your *it* trees
that framed our play
where we stood in captivity
holding each other hand to hand
like a string of paper dolls

I almost hear
the stifling of raw laughter
red-faced and mean-spirited
guffaws like an old man coughing

and our school marm placed
the filmy inflation
taking in a last big breath
like final wishes
as the milk-film translucence of that small zeppelin
filled her hands
and I cherish the charm of the virgin
the life-long chastity
of that dear woman
for whom we were all of us
her beloved children - every one
and I do not laugh
but smile

if I think
how last evening
in a poets' circle
we talked of Sir William Osler
that nineteenth century physician

who encouraged his medical students to pursue
*a clear mind and*
*a loving heart*
he who first saw
animalcules flowering on filmy glass
he who studied cadavers in the dead house
within the courtyard of the Blockley gardens
alive with yellow daffodils
in the Cotswold village
beside the pond
where the bronze statue of a young girl
pours out unceasing waters
from giving jug to
ever-receiving rippling pool

and if there is life eternal
in Osler's ashes
at old McGill
where all the equanimities
of one soul
radiate like the bell
we once heard
sounding over the land of our youth
calling us to attend
and give
obeisance to lost memory
as all learning *is* quintessential recall
of the already known

is it little wonder then
that I give Christ's benefit
to the lascivious and seemingly snide youth
hiding in the shadows of time
like everyone's dark companion

# Chapter 4: Caring for Humanity

*Sandra Ens*

When we talk about suffering, our natural inclination is to imagine the extremes: despair, devastation, or profound loss. It is the suffering we see on the nightly news of people in the most abject of circumstances, deprived of adequate water or food, homes destroyed by natural disasters or wars, forced to flee. We think of individual and personal examples of suffering: people we know who have lost children, who have nursed others through debilitating diseases, and who have experienced emotional trauma.

We rarely experience such dangers, threats, or anguish. The suffering most people experience is more a forbearance of people, events, and expectations in our daily lives; we use the word in such phrases as "she does not suffer fools gladly." Such suffering is less drastic but can nevertheless be debilitating because it is draining. When I thought about my suffering as a teacher, my first thought was, "I didn't suffer. What I experienced was not suffering." I received much the same response from other teachers I asked. What emerged was not so much a question of whether I suffered, but what was the nature of the suffering?

The relationship between teacher and student is often portrayed in books, plays, and movies, and it is often misrepresented and exaggerated. The teacher is very cool, or very strict, or very tolerant, extremes for dramatic effect. Students are initially difficult but eventually won over, reach

S. Ens (✉)
Calgary, AB, Canada

© The Author(s) 2019
S. Steel and A. Homeniuk (eds.),
*Suffering and the Intelligence of Love in the Teaching Life*,
https://doi.org/10.1007/978-3-030-05958-3_7

their potential, perform beautifully, and go on to stellar lives, all because of the teacher. A stark contrast to this romanticism is found in *Pygmalion* by George Bernard Shaw, in which Henry Higgins shows us the truth of what many teachers endure.

Awaiting a taxi after an evening at the opera, Henry cannot help himself; he takes notes of the various dialects and pronunciations that he hears, identifying correctly the influences on each accent. His comments are misunderstood and his knowledge is called into question. Most teachers experience the same suspicion because they appear to hold special knowledge, and those who don't have it feel intimidated by it. Henry studies accents, and his studies inform his teaching because teachers share their knowledge and expertise in order to improve the lives of their students. In this "age of upstarts,"[1] he teaches his students to speak with accents that will help them move up the social ladder. His vague contempt for the Eynsford-Hills reveals what many teachers feel: disdain for those who have abilities, gifts, brains, but fail to use them. Teaching Eliza articulate speech will rescue her from life in the gutter and fulfill her ambition of becoming a "lady in a flower shop."

The characters gathered around the opera house, many of them uneducated as portrayed by their rough accents, observe and criticize Henry. They have a few suggestions for how he should proceed. Teachers endure the scrutiny and interference by those who misunderstand the process and the system, misrepresentation by the media and the public, as well as decisions and influence made by those far from the classroom. We are required to put into practice curriculum changes without adequate resources; we attempt to integrate new technologies without time for proper in-service, and we work through new marks reporting programs only when our first evaluations must be entered. Mostly, it is someone's "Big Idea" that we are required to implement. Throughout my career, I often encountered these ambitious plans: A new English Language Arts curriculum, administrative and professional language about establishing a Community of Learners, the Alberta Initiative for School Improvement, mandated Daily Physical Activity (DPA), as well as the implementation of a School Education Plan and a Five-Year Business Plan. What happened to all these initiatives? They lacked appropriate funding to provide in-service, adequate acceptance and or adoption from teachers, and what was hoped for could not be accomplished. In theory, these are good ideas. In practice, schools struggle to make them work.

While changes have merit, they originate from criticism: what schools *should* be doing while ignoring what schools are *actually* doing. Most teachers would agree that some reform of the system is necessary, yet it is often those furthest from the classroom, those without educational background or with a specific agenda, who influence the direction of the reform. Some experts advocate for broader use of computers, others for job training. Cuts to education target "extras", even though we demand that schools allow students the freedom to pursue their own interests, and at the same time maintaining "high standards of excellence." Demands are high: Schools should teach sex education and financial literacy; they should offer daily physical education and fine arts, supply social worker liaison officers, and provide safe havens for GSAs. And do not, above all, abandon teaching "the basics". Yet what teachers know through experience and instinct often runs contrary to suggestions for reform. Technology cannot replace human interaction and direct assistance from a real person. The sole function of education should not be simply to train students for the workplace; it is essential to provide students with a breadth of experience. Change should not mollify ambitious parents who are focussed on achievement-oriented, quantifiable measures. Emotional and mental health services should not be considered "extras." Teachers are like other public professionals, such as nurses, of whom Margaret Atwood says, "Everyone expects so much of them and people beat up on them."[2] Criticism of teachers often comes from people who want their own needs met.

Henry encounters a neglectful parent in the unscrupulous Alfred Doolittle. After Alfred's bombastic entrance, demanding to see his daughter whose virtue he believes has been compromised, Henry naturally assumes Alfred will come regularly to see Eliza. He mentions to Doolittle, "It's your duty." But Alfred is evasive. He can't come "this week," saying, "I have a job at a distance; but you can depend upon me."[3] A vague promise followed by an excuse. But is the neglectful parent easier to deal with than the interfering parent? Alfred's absence is preferable to his presence—Henry would not have tolerated a parent sitting in on every lesson and observing his methods and would have bridled at sending daily reports on Eliza's progress.

When Higgins encounters a former student, Neppomuck, at the ambassador's garden party, he is met by the horror we all face: Neppomuck's belief that anybody can be a teacher. Even worse, Eliza later taunts Higgins with the threat: "I'll be a teacher. I'll offer myself as an assistant to [Neppomuck]."[4] The belief that anyone can teach ignores this: Good teaching is an art, not simply confined to imparting knowledge, and not easy to define. Students "know" who is a good teacher and who is not, even though teacher evaluation is often completed by checklist, which itemizes skills rather than acknowledging the art. I'm not even sure Henry *is* a good teacher: he bullies Eliza, assigns her homework after a long day of lessons, and dismisses her feelings.

What makes Henry admirable lies in the purity of his motives: Teaching would be impossible unless students are sacred. We enter the profession vowing to be the best teachers possible, but we are thwarted in that ideal by the circumstances we face. Class size and teaching load render it mostly impossible to meet the goals we set for ourselves. What we would like to do is conference with every student on each piece of writing, communicate regularly with parents about their children, maintain anecdotal records to provide feedback, and create interesting lessons that engage students. We hope to understand each student's diverse needs and address their learning styles with the appropriate teaching methods. While it is often rewarding, it is also a struggle to deal with the individual students in any given classroom. Coping with individual personalities is messy and unpredictable, and what works one day does not work the next. Students bring with them years of previous experience, multiple perceptions, and plenty of emotional baggage. Juggling the variables is wearing and exhausting. In order to achieve the sanctity of students, we need to consider the relationship between each individual and the curriculum; then we must plan flexibly so that each learner can be reflected in that curriculum. And we suffer the guilt because we are never able to meet our own expectations.

Those pure intentions are often misunderstood, unappreciated, and met with ingratitude. After the triumph of the ambassador's garden party, Shaw intends the audience to focus on Eliza's mood. She is hurt and angry because Higgins and Pickering do not acknowledge her hard work. But in this scene, Henry is also not appreciated. He reminds her: "I taught you everything you know," and "I've given you more than you've given me." When she is not suitably grateful, he feels as though he has "wasted his treasures."[5] Who receives the credit for success—student or teacher? And who incurs the blame for failure—student or teacher? Had Henry failed, had Eliza's deception been discovered, she still could have fulfilled her ambition of working in a flower shop, but Henry's reputation would have been ruined.

We are aware that our reputation as teachers lies the success of our students, yet we're overloaded with needs in the classroom. There may be six students with identified needs and individual educational plans. Often there are other students who have not been diagnosed, but who visibly struggle. The number and diversity of needs is growing in "average" students as well as among identified students. Nonetheless, we are expected to meet all those needs. We understand and appreciate the frustrations of parents with special needs students; we are likewise sympathetic to the frustrations of parents with children who we consider average, and who feel their needs are not being met. Teachers must teach every student in the class, and we are required to teach specific content and processes. But what is required of a teacher does not work for every student. Doing the best we can does not mean doing the best for every student.

Canada is one of the most diverse countries in the world. The demands on society are rapidly changing, and the demands on schools have grown as well. Teachers are very much trying to engage all students, but our pupils come from diverse experiences and cultures. Moreover, students each have specific interests and abilities: some prefer a quiet room, others a dynamic environment, which can be stressful for the former type of learner. And while education is mandatory until the age of sixteen, many students aren't interested in a course they're required to complete. We try to engage them, and to explain concepts in a way that they can all comprehend. What is reasonable to expect from a classroom teacher? Can we expect classroom teachers to be experts in their subject areas while at the same time being experts in learning disabilities, behaviour and anxiety disorders, mental and emotional health? Is it reasonable to expect that the classroom teacher can be everything to every student?

Ultimately, we still try, and we suffer the most when our students are suffering. Teachers who hesitate to talk about their own suffering talk about the suffering of specific students. Every teacher has stories about students who have challenges before they even arrive at school. We have taught students whose parents are divorcing, who suffer from depression and entertain thoughts of suicide, or those who have eating disorders. We have comforted students who have lost classmates or family members. When a child dies because of neglectful parents, or a teen suicide is revealed, I think about what those teachers tried to do for that student. When a tragic accident occurs on a field trip, when a truck runs into a busload of hockey players, I think of what that school community will endure. I know that those teachers will be called upon to provide support to students in the immediate aftermath as well as over many years. Those tragedies recur in the writing that students submit and in their discussion of text. For these students, we arrive early and stay late. It is these students we think about long after they've left our classrooms. It is for them we are willing to continue in a difficult and demanding profession because sometimes, we are the one person they need.

Is teaching a profession worth pursuing? Is it possible to cope? Yes, through the development of patience, forbearance, tolerance and acceptance of the difficulties of the profession. What Henry Higgins shows us is what all teachers know: Our deepest desire for our students is that they become independent. Putting aside his anger at Eliza for threatening to become a teacher and undercutting him, he recognizes that her threat is a plan for her own future, and he is triumphant. "Five minutes ago, you were a millstone around my neck. Now you're a tower of strength."[6] The conclusion of the play is not a conclusion at all. No graduation, no great success, no accolades. Eliza fulfills her ambition to work in a flower shop; she marries Freddy, and she also remains living with Higgins and Pickering. Not very satisfying, is it? Not as a romantic plot. But it is wholly satisfying when we recognize, as Eliza does, Henry's nature and motivation: He is a teacher because he cares for humanity, and that it is through education that true democracy and equality is achieved. Henry is like all teachers: We view our schools as environments in which all children belong, and in which each student is valued.

## Notes

1. Bernard Shaw, *Pygmalion* (London: Penguin Books, 1914), 26.
2. In Valerie Fortney, "Fortney: Literary icon Margaret Atwood on floods, fires and compassion" (*Calgary Herald*, May 28, 2016), http://calgaryherald.com/news/local-news/fortney-literary-icon-margaret-atwood-on-floods-fires-and-compassion.
3. Shaw, *Pygmalion*, 64.
4. Ibid., 138.
5. Ibid., 134.
6. Ibid., 139.

## References

Fortney, Valerie. "Fortney: Literary icon Margaret Atwood on floods, fires and compassion" (*Calgary Herald*, May 28 2016), http://calgaryherald.com/news/local-news/fortney-literary-icon-margaret-atwood-on-floods-fires-and-compassion.

Shaw, Bernard. *Pygmalion*. London: Penguin Books, 1914.

# Chapter 5: I Can't Believe It Myself Most Days …

*John B. Lee*

*"Teachers must no longer be the sage on the stage.
Now we must become the guide by the side." She intoned.*

*"What about the goof
on the roof?" He inquired.*

*(An exchange between a pedagogue seeing herself as bringing the tablets down from the mountain, and a mischief-maker at the end of a presentation during a secondary school staff meeting.)*

---

I dedicate this personal essay to the wonderful teachers and mentors of my youth—to all my teachers in general and in particular to my grade-school principal Miss Myrtle Downie, my grade XII English teacher Walter Cooper, my secondary school history teacher Mr. James She, my university instructors Stan Dragland and James Reaney, my Althouse professor Don Gutteridge, my classmate fellow-poet the career English teacher Roger Bell and to my publisher and friend Marty Gervais from whom I continue to learn and to my wife Cathy with whom I share my life.

---

J. B. Lee (✉)
Port Dover, ON, Canada

The last time I saw my grade eight teacher Miss Myrtle Downie, former principal of SS No 12, the three-room elementary school I attended in the village of Highgate, I had already been a secondary school teacher of English, Dramatic Arts, and Creative Writing at a six-hundred pupil rural school in Waterford, Ontario for almost a decade. I hadn't seen her since graduation day in 1965 when I was a callow lad on the cusp of thirteen, and she was an ancient lady most likely in her late forties or early fifties. Now she lived in the same retirement residence as my maternal grandmother. I was very glad to see her. I had apologies to make. She smiled at me from the comfort of her small room, looked me hard in the eye and said, "John, you look so natural."

I had grown my hair long as soon as I left the farm. My hair had begun to curl when puberty struck and by the time I started university I quit using hair tonics to tame my tresses and let my 'freak flag fly'. One of my great heroes was the famous electric guitar virtuoso and force of nature, Jimi Hendrix. I'd far rather have had hair like Paul McCartney, but that just wasn't the coiffure for me with my wild doo. I let it grow and fate decided my natural curl would morph into an Afro. If I tell people now, "I once had an Afro that would fill a doorway," they look at me with disbelief and laugh to imagine. Little wonder matronly Myrtle Downie would be so open with an offhand compliment. Or so I took it. "You look so natural," she'd said smiling. And I'd thanked her for that. She continued briefly, holding my gaze with hers, "I never thought that you, of all people, would ever become a teacher. I thought you hated teachers." And I realized as she said this, that she meant that she had thought I hated teachers in general and her in particular. I suppose the evidence of my conduct as a very immature and slightly smart alecky pipsqueak, a bespectacled Poindexter of slight stature, unathletic, feckless, and sickly with an unruly lickspittle cowlick sproinging out of my crown like a busted spring on a head-sized clock must have suggested an antipathy for pedagogues.

To tell the truth I didn't hate teachers and I certainly never held her in contempt. I do remember one particular day when I was showing off for the girls, trying to get a laugh during story time. Ironically, I loved story time. And if I recall correctly, the story teacher was reading from that day was *The Jungle Book*, by Rudyard Kipling. Every school day following afternoon recess Miss Downie would read to us for fifteen minutes or so. And I loved those sessions. Being read to from a classic is one of my elementary school favourite recollections. And Kipling's novel was something of an apotheosis from those halcyon occasions.

That said, my good friend Gerald Grant and I would often compete with one another showing off and trying to get the other to laugh and maybe even descend into fits of giggles. I suppose I must have been pulling faces, and whispering silly things, juking and engaging in general hijinks all without gaining the attention of teacher who was reading to us from the front of the room. Miss Downie finally had had enough of me. I had failed to remain sufficiently intrepid. She snapped shut her book and stamped her foot like an angry ewe warning I'd come too close to the lamb. She called my name and pointed over her shoulder to the door at the front of the classroom leading into the small bookroom where all who went there knew the axiom *'Abandon hope all ye who enter here,'* for this instruction bore the consequence of a verdict. This was where you went to receive *the strap*.

I was of the 'spare the rod and spoil the child' generation. I had received the strap any number of times in the early years of my first instruction. My best friend in grade one Dicky Lewyll had received the strap so often the palms of his hands were weathered like old paint. And I had grown accustomed to the red sting often enough to avoid provoking the need. That day in grade eight would be the first occasion in many years that I would be found worthy of anything so Draconian. I obeyed Miss Downie. I walked tuck tailed and dutifully into the torture chamber. She pulled the door shut leaving me alone inside. "I'll be there in a minute," she said. And there I stood in that bookish silence surrounded by volumes I'd read and some I had not. I loved the school-bus yellow pile of *National Geographic*, the ones the eldest Roust boy used to read hard-swallowing a half-chewed wad of his fried-egg sandwich all the while thumbing the pages as he gulped. I can still almost smell the yolky fragrance of fried eggs and hard globs of country butter whenever I behold an uncut *Geographic*.

Time passed like the slow drip of a leaf tip in a light rain. Silence dried the air in that dry-aired room. The doorknob turned. The door creaked open. And Miss Myrtle Downie entered and closed the silence behind her. There we two were, cramped in that small room—I with my shame; she with her stern intent. And then she said simply, "You aren't a bad boy, Johnny. I'm sure you'll be better behaved in future. Let us never speak of this again."

I do not recall what I said. I only recall that for the first time in my life I realized that teachers were human. I realized that she suffered to think of giving the strap as much as I suffered to anticipate the hot sting of it being administered.

So that day years later in the retirement home when she'd said to me, "I thought you hated teachers," I wanted to throw my arms about her and to embrace her and to say, "No! I didn't hate teachers. I didn't even know that teachers were human. I used to think that when teachers left the school they went home and hung their bodies on wooden hangers like mothy overcoats, or tossed themselves in chairs like drop-stringed marionettes. Teachers didn't eat or sleep or play. In summer they estivate like woolens in a cedar trunk. I didn't hate teachers. And I certainly didn't hate you."

We sipped our tea that day as equals. I in my Afro and she in her faux pearls and teacher shoes with coffee mug heels, two teachers taking our ease. I didn't know it then, but I would defenestrate after only fourteen years in the classroom. Although I enjoyed my profession, I preferred writing to teaching and the opportunity to become a full-time writer presented itself in my life. And so, I jumped out the window and fled the profession in my early thirties.

Now, I'm sixty-four and since I left full-time teaching in the summer of 1990, I've had ample opportunity to keep my oar in the water. I've done workshops in writing from kindergarten through grade thirteen. I've taught neophytes barely beginning their alphabet and advanced writers with many books to their credit. I've lectured all over the world. I've taught literature at several universities and been the guest of English Departments from Maine to Wisconsin to Nelson Mandela's alma mater Witwatersrand in Johannesburg, South Africa. I've served as writer in residence at several universities and in several libraries. And I've learned a few things that I take to heart. *Never steal anyone's joy* is my major credo; and *better a bad poem than a good bomb* my Cri de Coeur.

\*   \*   \*

Unlike me, my wife spent her entire working life as a teacher except for brief interruptions due to maternity leaves and the vicissitudes of ill health. I became a teacher of necessity. What else might an English major do? Although I would argue that she was far more naturally suited to becoming a great teacher than I, Cathy followed me into the profession the September after we were married. We came home from our honeymoon in late summer 1974, walked into the admissions office at Althouse College, and threw ourselves on the mercy of the administrator saying, "We'd like to go here." It was a Friday afternoon and classes began on the following Monday morning. I enrolled in English and Dramatic Arts, and she enrolled in Physical Education and Guidance. Eight months later, just short of graduation, we were hired at Waterford District High School, both of us in our areas of specialization. Two years later we had permanent contracts. I taught for fourteen years until I defenestrated in favour of becoming a full-time writer. Although I went on to life as a somewhat peripatetic instructor, it was Cathy whose career in teaching was varied and challenging.

After teaching secondary school for ten years, in 1984 she was seconded to the W. Ross MacDonald School for the Visually Impaired in Brantford where she taught for several years while acquiring her specialist in Blind Education. Then she was hired by the Brantford Board of Education as teacher of elementary school students who were in trouble with the law. In the meantime, she acquired her specialist in special education and her specialist in primary education and thereby became qualified to teach children with special needs and she spent the remainder of her career in several schools in the city teaching students who were identified. She came home with stories to tell and it was her career that inspired me to coin the phrase "I can't believe myself most days," to describe her experiences in the system.

She always treated her students with utmost respect and kindness. She championed their immediate needs and was a vigilant advocate on behalf of their long-term educational prospects. Many, though not all of them, were from disadvantaged homes. The worst winter of her career came as something of a nadir that is so awful to consider it seems impossible to believe. She was teaching in a school situated in a relatively affluent suburban region of the city. You might imagine that her principal would be sympathetic to the plight of her students since he was on a committee founded to advocate on behalf of the poor. This could not have been further from the truth.

The poverty level of her students was such that several of them did not own winter coats, boots, hats, or mittens. One poor lad did not even own a pair of socks. In the fall she had been assigned a classroom in a portable outside the boundaries of the school building. She would often arrive to find one of her students there, seated on the steps, shivering in a thin jacket, waiting for her to open her door. Just before Christmas vacation, one of the parent volunteers who worked at Walmart as a manager convinced the store to donate clothing for her students. She gave them each a toque, mittens, a scarf and two pair of socks, along with candy and a toy. The boys and girls gobbled up the candy, paid brief attention to the toy, but they were absolutely thrilled by the winter clothing. For some of them it would be the first mittens they had ever owned.

After Christmas vacation the students arrived in the portable to discover that the heating system had broken down over the holiday. When Cathy brought this to the attention of the principal, she was told to tough it out until the problem was solved. The temperature plunged and when it became unbearable to stay put, she brought her students into the school library where she set up class. The principal found out and told her to go back to the portable where her class belonged. They sat in the portable like orphans in the gulags of the Soviet, keeping warm by wearing winter apparel all day. When she approached her union representative to advocate on her behalf, she was told to follow orders. When she wrote a letter to the health and safety commission, the letter was intercepted and she was warned that if she persisted in her efforts she would be *written up* for insubordination and a letter would be put on file as the first step in the process toward dismissal. She had no recourse but to suffer, and to allow her students to suffer on for the entire month of January waiting for the janitorial staff to repair the heating system. This may seem so Dickensian as to make it sound like something right out of a nineteenth century novel. But this was the decade of Mike Harris when war was being waged on the poor. Little wonder I coined the phrase *I can't believe it myself most days?* Even as I write this I find myself thinking "Surely I'm exaggerating. Surely this cannot be true." Had I not witnessed it myself, I might be skeptical.

During her stint in the next school, a core city school with nothing like the resources that were available in middleclass regions of the city, she experienced deprivations on a school-wide basis that did not occur in her previous school. When the student washrooms ran out of soap and paper towel, the bathrooms went without being stocked for the remainder of the term. When the classrooms supplies were used up, they were not replenished. The Parents' Council in poorer neighbourhoods was able to make only very modest amounts of money through fund raising. One scheme involved a breakfast program for students. The food was donated by charity, the staff cooked the breakfast, and each student was asked to sign up for the program that cost twenty-five cents a week. When Cathy collected the money from her students she noticed that one of her most deserving children had not signed up for the breakfast. "Jimmy," she said. "You should sign up for this breakfast." "I can't miss," he said. "And why not?" She inquired. "My mom doesn't have twenty-five cents, miss."

That very morning I had heard a man interviewed on the radio saying he always sends his Versace socks to the dry cleaners. Versace Medusa Men's Navy-Gold Dress Socks retail at $26.99 American a pair. Only the day before a Russian oil tycoon had spent $52,000 on lunch at a posh restaurant in Manhattan. Is it little wonder I write *I can't believe it myself most days?*

But I do believe it. I believe it because it is true. I believe because it happened in my city in my lifetime on my watch within my experience as a teacher in a system that claims to be one of the best in the world. I always said of myself that I would create an oasis of excellence in my classroom. However pretentious that may sound, I dedicated myself to that ideal. Whatever else was going on in the world; whatever else went on outside my door, I would create an environment where children were safe and where together we might manage to take seriously the business at hand. I know that children suffer. Growing up is hard enough work. The best teachers are amongst the greatest champions of youth. And I have known some of the best teachers. Miss Myrtle Downie who came into our grade seven classroom to tell us that President John F. Kennedy had been shot gave us that news with a quavering voice because she cared profoundly about our young lives and she knew that we needed the reassurance that we are all in the same boat. Even in this 'I can't believe it myself most days' world, we are not alone. We are in the company of great teachers whose compassionate guidance we might feel even in our own later years. I can believe, and I do believe in a better world, an oasis of excellence, a place we might share even if only in a dream.

PART III

# East-Meets-West: Finding Rhythms and Articulating Meaning in Suffering

# ode to the critic
# (or what was I trying to say?

*Daniela Elza*

his eyebrows raised                for lack of

commas.           his punctual gaze
piercing       the spaces      I have left

              (here          the breath
cannot be steady      as the hands
of clocks or     accurate     as dials.

           (this gap
           this pause is

for the reader.
              is where we walk
and our footprints will not     leave a trace.

---

D. Elza (✉)
Vancouver, BC, Canada
e-mail: daniela@livingcode.org

© The Author(s) 2019
S. Steel and A. Homeniuk (eds.),
*Suffering and the Intelligence of Love in the Teaching Life*,
https://doi.org/10.1007/978-3-030-05958-3_9

yet     if we are to trace     what thought
moves here—
            a rugged mountainous landscape

the mind endlessly explores       to find
a quiet temple where the silence gathers

so big     it cannot leave     the mouth.
                    *

here ambiguity proliferates
                what a comma clarifies

and shuts the door I have left (on purpose)
            open.

a clarity that does not     raise eyebrows
does not     take your breath away.

what informs the words       is the gap
through which we come     to a place

            of wor(d)ship

settle down and rise         through
            its paper thin silence

where thought grows deep.

            and then this (dream

we are
        both dreaming
on the page.     is it the cause     or
is it the result?     the left out comma is

            a door
                *

through which you do not walk inside

## 9 ODE TO THE CRITIC (OR WHAT WAS I TRYING TO SAY?

my head      but inside      yourself

       (seeking.     and in an image
or a word apart from others     (finding

(losing     yourself
in such needed     reverie
       in such a state of     emergence

that you should never fear     you are
misreading me.

---

First published in *Poetic Inquiry: Vibrant Voices in the Social Sciences* (Sense Publishers, The Netherlands, 2009). Poem reprinted with permission from author.

# Chapter 6: Suffering and the Blues

*Harry Manx*

When some people hear about the Blues they think of the usual clichés. They see a guy whose dog bit him, or whose wife left him. But in fact, the Blues is another way of saying that you're suffering. And because of that, there's nobody that hasn't experienced the Blues. It's a household phenomenon. The Blues is about life-sized struggles and pain, and it must be seen as spiritual music for that reason. It is Man seeking release from his pain and suffering. Music has not only the potential to transform your life; it has the power to help you overcome the hard times and the dark misery of your days.

Blues music was not created to please the masses, to make somebody rich, or to be the latest disposable fashion. It is the direct voice of the human spirit. Although not every musician who plays the Blues will grasp the depth of this music, each will bring whatever they have, whoever they are, and wherever they've been to their playing. They will at least contribute their own story.

My music is a reflection of my life's journey. The notes I choose speak to my creativity which has its source in my life experiences. Some of the notes I choose sound like the India I know from a dozen years of living there. The people, sights, sounds, and smells of India are all expressed in my music.

---

H. Manx (✉)
Salt Spring Island, BC, Canada

© The Author(s) 2019
S. Steel and A. Homeniuk (eds.),
*Suffering and the Intelligence of Love in the Teaching Life*,
https://doi.org/10.1007/978-3-030-05958-3_10

I sat at the feet of a living Buddha in India for many years. His words are reflected in my words. When I studied with a Master Musician in Rajasthan, his sound became my sound. But the emotions driving my music, the emotions that I bring, I didn't get from anyone else. They have their roots in the struggles I've personally encountered in my own life journey. All the suffering that I went through that was literally life changing is contained in my songs.

Other combinations of notes that I'm attracted to sound like the Blues. There's something very "gut feeling" and intuitive about expressing your own story through the Blues that attracts me. As a musician, obviously, it doesn't help to intellectualize your experiences. Listeners won't buy into it. They'll love you more if you sing about what a mess you're in and, "Oh Lord, won't you help me!" Audiences want you to let it hang out, and they want to hear how you have been run over by the tough lessons of life. Then they'll feel like they know you, and they'll be connected to you through suffering.

You'll hear many Blues songs about the world of love and relationships. That's the first story of suffering that seems to be on the minds of many Blues players. It's the most common theme; after all, who hasn't suffered at the hands of love? We all have, and it's comforting to know that you're not the only "fool for love" out there. But when it comes to telling my stories in song, I prefer to let suffering inform the music rather than sing a song about suffering. I let suffering give a greater depth and meaning to the words. I don't want to bring my listeners down; that's not the goal for me. I don't want to use my songs in a cathartic capacity either. I want my music to be more objective than that. I like to paint an optimistic and inspiring picture. But without having gone through my own suffering, I doubt that my words or my music would have the weight needed to move people. There's a subtle authority to a voice that speaks with the depth of suffering contained within it. Our words are qualified by the wisdom we gain through painful experiences. There seems to be no way around suffering; if you become stuck in it, chances are it's a downward slope. But if you get through it, there's a whole new world on the other side. Take Blues musicians, for instance: they've been singing about their troubles for a long while; they've grown to know their troubles, and having learned to accept the things that can't be changed, they've moved on—probably to new troubles, but that's what we do.

As listeners to the Blues, you may hear *the musician* in the music. You might hear his troubles and his take on life. But you might also learn about yourself because in listening to someone sing the Blues, you may feel like you're listening to someone singing your own story. You might feel something deep moving in you that needs expression. You may even feel like singing or playing music yourself once you see that singing out your suffering can be beautiful, inspired, pure, and transformational. Like a lot of music, mine is aimed at the Heart. I want to reach people in a way that bypasses intellectual processes. To that end, I don't inject the songs with opinions, judgements, or complaints. In fact, anything that would cause the audience to listen in a way that activates their reasoning minds or that prompts a discursive, intellectual response, I leave out. I keep the sounds and words poetic, mystical, and mysterious, out there in the realm of the Unknown, and in a place where thinking gives way to feeling and sensing. This is where music can transform the listener to a place of healing, letting go, and waking up. This may sound pretty esoteric, but the fact is that very few people understand the physical power that music has over us. Some great research has been done by people like Daniel Levitin in his book *This Is Your Brain on Music*. The evidence is there; the Blues is big medicine. Like Muddy Waters sings, it gets your mojo working!

You might ask how I'm able to communicate with so many people and to build musical connections with them even though most of those people aren't like me very much at all. How does it work? We all come from such very different life backgrounds; we have so many different ideas and views about the world. In conversation, we'd probably never agree with half the folks who attend the same concert. And yet, when we go to a musical event, there is such a great communal feeling there sometimes. How does music cut through all the differences to what is *common* among us? Does that have something to do with suffering, and how all of us suffer?

Is there a healing power in music that can help us get over our differences and animosities? And how does the consummate musician take the suffering, longing, or whatever-it-is in the music and channel that successfully to create gratitude, health, or hope in his or her audience?

All these questions point to one thing: *with respect to our discriminating minds, we are all separate; but in our hearts we are all one*. We're all one in that we have shared experiences, many of which are painful and involve suffering, but these experiences can teach us empathy and compassion towards others in a way that rational argumentation cannot. As we learn by means of our own suffering, this helps us to know what the pain of others feels like. However, all of these experiences are in the realm of the Heart. There's no way to speak about these things without it sounding a bit like unprovable, new-age mumbo jumbo, but there's no denying what everyone already senses: that there's a great deal of mysterious cause and effect happening in and around music. There's a lot we don't understand, or perhaps accept. But it's there, and the impact of music on our thoughts and emotions is undeniable. I can see my crowd moved to tears. Later when I meet them, they tell me how the music changed their lives. I know what they mean; I have my artists that do that for me. It's a big mystery that I don't try to solve.

One thing I realized many years ago is that people crave connection; this is perhaps why they like people with stories that are similar to their own. Because of this desire for community and connection, some artists whose message includes a kind of suffering that great numbers of people can identify with become very popular. Striking this universal chord with an audience can be challenging, however, because although we all suffer, we do so in a host of different ways; moreover, because our suffering is an internal process, it might not be obvious so we don't always notice each other's pain. Our pain remains hidden, and we suffer in alienation. Our suffering may be physical, emotional, or psychological, but suffering of this kind serves to drag us down in the end. Without relation or community, our suffering takes the shine off living; it sends humour into a dormant state, and creativity is virtually non-existent. This state of being, this dark malady, and this emptiness is what they call having "the Blues."

So the Blues is a kind of sickness at Heart; but as an art form, the Blues is simultaneously the cure to this malady. The Blues is a song about hard times. Born historically out of the African slaves' struggle towards freedom in America, it was a way to express the pain of living. That was the song they felt inspired to sing. Voicing that pain became a cure for what ailed them. Singing the Blues was a way to let their suffering go. Blues musicians have known for a long time that the Blues is both the cure and the illness. Although the lyrics of many Blues tunes describe painful experiences, the music is often delivered with a deep musical groove that turns the words on their head, helping the listener to let go of the suffering. You may hear a Blues singer letting loose about suffering and hard times, and all the while your toe can't stop itself from tapping. That's the alchemy of the Blues, taking a negative (suffering) experience and transforming it into a song, a dance, a poem—helping you to move on.

Of course, most people don't want to have the Blues or to suffer. In fact, they want to avoid it at all costs. But for all the misery and discomfort that suffering brings, there seems to be an upside too. I have noticed in myself and others that people can grow through the insights they glean from their exposure to pain and suffering. The learning we do through exposure to the pains of life is transformational. Suffering is one of those things that you can't un-do, un-see, un-feel, un-realize once you've felt it. Your being adjusts its perspective on everything to include the "pain perspective."

Mind you: suffering isn't a form of education that I'd recommend for just anyone. Although suffering can ennoble and teach, it can also have the effect of destroying inspiration. Chances are pretty good that eventually it will. Especially when it seems to have no meaning or purpose, suffering can rob you of your desire and your ability to be creative. It can put you in a place where the only thing you have to share is a destructive perspective. You begin to reflect the world in all its perceived ugliness. Any growth that happens through pain and suffering is simply the silver lining of a crappy situation.

You don't necessarily need suffering to grow wise, either, but I think that suffering can bring out resources in us that we didn't know we had. We learn something else about ourselves in painful situations that we wouldn't have learned in a safe environment. We tap into different strengths to deal with the suffering. Without suffering, we might not change the course of our lives. We may not want to fix what's not broken. If you could pull far back and see your whole life's journey in one continuous stream you might see that without suffering you would have had an entirely different journey through life.

Many artists have lived their lives on the edge of self-inflicted pain and suffering, driven by booze, drugs, and excitement. For some people, this is probably the "zone" where they feel the most inspired, totally alive, and ready to entertain the public. It appears that pleasure blocks their creativity, but pain clears the way for inspiration. Anyone wanting to be creative and expressive finds this out very quickly, and will endeavour to invite an appropriate amount of suffering in order to drive their inspiration forward. If you are a professional musician, painter, dancer, or writer, it just might be to your advantage to have a measured amount of suffering propelling your desire to express it.

Finding our way out of suffering is one of the most basic themes in songs, films, and stories of all kinds. It's at the heart of stories depicting the struggle of good against evil, as well as in more innocent tales of girl-meets-boy. It's an important part of the "story of the hero" who overcomes adversity and suffering to achieve his goals. Some say that's the basic theme of all stories: overcoming the Blues. In the world of art and music, no one is more loved than the person who overcomes suffering to achieve great goals in his or her work. "From rags to riches" stories—whether the wealth be coined in gold or in goods of the spirit—makes a great impression on most people. We all want to overcome the Blues—if not in our own lives, then we like to hear of someone else doing it.

One lesson that I've learned and tried to teach in the context of my art is that, although living in suffering may help people to achieve their ambitions, and although it might fuel their careers or inflate their egos, without cultivating self-knowledge, they find themselves unable to move through their suffering to a better place. A little education in self-awareness could go a long way to helping such people. Saying "No" to beauty in your art or your life in general is primal behaviour; like a baby throwing a tantrum, it's the domain of the unconscious mind—that mind which skitters along the surface of things plotting and managing daily affairs in terms of our thoughts, fears, desires, and ambitions without connection or insight grounded in the kind of Heart-knowing that is cultivated in music. The simple path to reversing such difficulties is to say: "I accept that I create and maintain most of my own suffering; therefore, I'm also the (only) one who can un-create it."

Here's my approach to transforming my own suffering into a state of natural joy: I recognize it; I accept that it is happening; I watch it; it passes.

At some point in my life I made it a point to play music that would reflect my inner world.

Music is my meditation. When I play, I have to be in the moment. When I play from that place, I play with totality and abandonment. The music is there, my mind not so much. My Guru in India told me to "never be greater than the music. Be at your best, in your heart when playing because the listener will be able to hear what's in your heart, what's in your soul, what you feel.... it will come through your fingers. If you are living in suffering and pain, you will play that and the audience will feel it. Choose wisely what message you want to convey."

## Reference

Levitin, Daniel. *This Is Your Brain on Music: The Science of a Human Obsession.* Dutton, 2007.

# *it:* attempts at definition

## *Daniela Elza*

it comes willing          and open.
leaves closed with brass hinges and a lock.
teacher says:     *now*      *you have the key.*

      \*

it's the cherry blossoms          falling
against the tick-      tock    of the hands
the petal's thought       against the cheek.

      \*

it worships with the certainty of   a needle
pulling      the thread        through.

      \*

at university they said       they will not
take my word    for    *it.*   they took cash
and two pieces of ID     instead.

      \*

it cannot follow the recipe because it *knows*
what it should not          leave out.

*

it writes pages      by moonlight
wants to craft            a word
         full of   moon.

*

it resists having       its picture taken
'cause      it is not a thousand words
or more              or less.

*

it divides and multiplies the numbers on its ID.

*

it cannot tell you      what it means
'cause it feeds its words to       the crows
and forgets them in the hollows of     trees.

*

it is every poem      but
every poem       is not it.

*

once transformed it turns you into
another door       another threshold of
blue or yellow.

*

It thinks it is       rational
constantly finds itself    *relational*.

*

it tears recipes out of a book
eats them
because it took their words for   *it*.

*

it often sleeps in the pockets of children.
and when they pull it out
to show you    how its fur shines
you are ashamed    for not believing.

excerpt from   *the book of it* by Daniela Elza (2011)

First published in *the weight of dew* (Mother Tongue Publishing, 2012). Poem reprinted with permission from author.

# Chapter 7: Ajahn Chah Gives a Teaching

*Tim Ward*

There is only one thing left to be done. Ruk agrees to be my companion and on the appointed day we begin the three-hour walk to visit Wat Pah Pong, where I will bow three times before Ajahn[1] Chah, the monk whose books and reputation led me to Pah Nanachat. Ruk comes not only as my guide, because I don't know the way, nor just because his company along the twelve-kilometre walk will be a joy. He is the one disciple of the master who seems to reflect some of the holiness I would expect to find in the great teacher. Ruk's words and stories about Ajahn Chah are full of gentle devotion. I fear my own aversion could rear up suddenly like a viper if I go alone. I don't want that. I am not visiting to pass judgment, only to pay my respects, as a pupil to a master. I wonder if the Ajahn has a teaching left for me.

Ruk leads me through Bung Wai village and across a set of railway lines. We walk down along a maze of country trails. The sky is clear, except for a few dark clouds boiling on the horizon. The breeze is fair.

---

Excerpt from Tim Ward, *What the Buddha Never Taught* (Berkeley: Celestial Arts Publishing, 1990), 271–281.

---

T. Ward (✉)
Bethesda, MD, USA

It keeps us from wilting under the hot afternoon sun. Ruk is true to his name. His conversation fills us both with laughter. He tells me stories about the villages we pass, about the strange and colourful crops in the fields, about Thai monks he has known and about the history of our destination, Wat Pah Pong.

"Ajahn Chah was born in a village near where the *wat*[2] is now. His family still lives there. For fifteen years he wandered through the countryside. Most of the time he spent in deep jungle, meditating. One day, he came back to this area and went to stay in the old cremation grounds to practise."

"Old cremation grounds seem like a popular spot for monks," I add.

"They are really popular. Most villagers are afraid of the ghosts, so they are good for solitude."

"Every monastery should enlist the aid of *peepahs*."[3]

"Word soon got around that the famous forest monk had returned. The villagers asked him if they could build a monastery for him and the small group of disciples who followed him. Ajahn Chah didn't object, so they built Pah Pong around him. By the time he had his stroke, he had forty branch monasteries all over Thailand."

"They say there's over sixty now."

Before we can begin a discussion on the merit of monastery building, we reach a three-metre high concrete wall at the end of our trail.

"It looks like a prison," I say to Ruk as we pass through a large iron door. Ruk tells me it's the back entrance to the grounds of Pah Pong. Inside, a two-metre high cement wall runs along the right side of a dirt road. It continues straight ahead for a kilometer, out of sight. On the left, a barbed-wire fence protects dense forest. It feels eerie.

"I doubt if Ajahn Chah would have designed it this way himself," says Ruk as we begin to walk alongside the inner wall.

After half a kilometer we come to a wooden ladder leaning against the wall. I follow Ruk up it and down another one on the other side. A dog-proof entrance to the main grounds. The trees are thinner here. As we approach an open grassy area ahead, I notice dozens of wooden *kuties*[4] raised on stilts. Unlike the ones at Pah Nanachat, there is no attempt to isolate the huts from one another. It looks like a monastic suburb. A few Thais in ochre robes watch us as we pass. Ruk leads me to the *sala*.[5] From the outside, the temple looks like a curling rink with a corrugated tin roof. Inside, it can easily accommodate five hundred worshippers. The floor is covered with old patches of linoleum of different colours and patterns. Incense burns before the giant brass Buddhas on the altar. Human skeletons encased in glass stand in each front corner. A double suicide?

A monk arrives who recognizes Ruk. They speak together in Thai for a few minutes. Ruk carries with him a pile of visa renewal forms sent by our Ajahn to the senior monk at Pah Pong. They will be sent to Bangkok for processing. Pah Pong handles all the paperwork for Pah Nanachat's *farang*[6] monks. The Thai tells Ruk that the elder is at Ajahn Chah's bungalow. The master himself will receive visitors only between five and six p.m., when he is taken out in his wheelchair.

It is too early to go, so we stroll through the vast grounds of the *wat*. We pass a new bell tower six storeys tall, built in an ancient baroque style. Carved deities, demons and gargoyles stare down at us. Near a glade, large rock totems jut up from the carefully trimmed grass. Ruins from the cremation site. Further on is a small green hill which slopes gently upward to the new *bot*.[7] Ruk tells me the hill is man-made, a huge underground water tank, kept full as a reserve for the dry season. The *bot* is modern, completed less than two years ago. Its smooth white lines soar upwards gracefully like an abstract sculpture. We climb the white stone steps. It awes me that such a building could be created in Thailand. The ceiling is composed of white arches. The walls are semi-open, made up of large relief mosaics depicting scenes from the life of Ajahn Chah. In one, a king cobra peacefully crosses his path; in another, two tigers observe him with respect as he sits in deep contemplation; in a third, villagers build a forest *kuti* for him while he blesses them; in the fourth, the master sits alone in *samadhi*.[8] The front of the *bot* has about an eight-metre high statue in grey metal of a standing Buddha, both arms raised at right angles from the elbows. It's an unusual posture for a Buddha. Beneath the idol and slightly in front of it on the floor is a life-sized statue of a monk. The iron figure sits crosslegged in Thai meditation posture, right leg resting on top of the left. The toes of the right foot arch casually upwards. He is a relaxed-looking old man, perhaps a little tired. His lips turn down slightly at the corners, yet the expression is not dour. Somehow it seems like a smile. The artists gave the piece a rough texture, creating a harmonious contrast with the sleek modern lines of the *bot*. We kneel and bow three times to the Buddha and three times to the statue of Ajahn Chah.

Leaving the *bot*, we walk back past the *sala* and down a long road to the front gate of the *wat*. Pah Pong's boundaries are wide, more than two kilometers from end to end. The place seems strangely empty, ghost-like. Ruk tells me there were over sixty Thai and *farang* monks in Pah Pong when he came four years ago. Now there are fewer than ten, although more will return for *pansa*.[9] The walk to the gate takes us through another tall forest. Painted signs written in Thai are nailed to trees next to the road. Ruk explains that they are sayings from the *Dhamma*.[10] One-liner *dasanas*[11] for visitors.

"Some monks think even the trees should have a teaching for us here," says Ruk. It is difficult to tell if he speaks with irony.

> Wooden signs are tacked to trees
> For those who cannot read.

We pass through the inner gate. In front of us is a building under construction. The foundation is complete. Wooden beams have been erected over it. To one side is a hill of bamboo which will be used as scaffolding. Beyond, there is an outer gate with an iron door next to it. Through the gate I see a small and rickety shack. I know it's a noodle shop. I have been here before, the night I searched so long in the dark and rain for the place which was now my home.

"What are they building?" I asked Ruk. "When I last saw it, it was just a big hole."

"It's a museum."

"A museum? I thought you said the monastery was built when the master got here. It's not so old. A museum—Ruk, you mean a mausoleum. It's for Ajahn Chah, isn't it? The main attraction will be his ashes. Or will they goldplate him and set him on display? The teacher isn't even dead and already they are setting up the market to make money from his relics." Anger flares inside. I don't want it to strike out at my gentle friend. "Tell me, am I wrong to think such negative things? What do you think? Are they just keeping his body breathing for the sake of the merit industry?" I feel as cynical as Jim.

"His disciples love him very much," says the monk in a soft voice. "You can't expect them to let him die. Some days I think he has very clear eyes. See for yourself."

We walk along the outside of the wall to a corner. Around it to the right, about four hundred meters away, is a bungalow. Three or four clusters of monks sit at various places on the green lawn surrounding it.

Several cars and a few vans are parked in a nearby lot. Moving slowly around the perimeter of the building is a small figure in an orange-ochre robe, slumped in a wheelchair. A second figure pushes the chair around a cement strip which encircles the house. A third, also in a monk's robe, carries a long-handled fan which he waves over the one in the chair.

We leave our sandals near the front gate of the bungalow, pass through and follow the walkway to the rear of the building. An attendant novice motions us to sit on the grass. We wait for the wheelchair to come around to us. The threesome rounds the corner at a slow speed. I follow Ruk's example and kneel as the slumped figure in the chair approaches. We press our palms together in a respectful *wai*.[12] The novice pushing the chair halts in front of us. We bow three times, touching our foreheads to the grass.

Ajahn Chah's eyes are closed, his head fallen to the side. It leans against the back of the wheelchair. The lower jaw is slack. The mouth hangs open at an unnatural angle, forming a triangle from which a pale tongue protrudes. White spittle covers the corners of the lips. The attendant keeps a cloth ready which he uses to wipe away the drool from the master's chin. The old hands are folded one on top of the other. They are mottled and pale for a Thai. The right one twitches occasionally like a dying fish. This is the only movement other than the gentle heaving of the great and collapsing chest buried beneath the robes. I hear him groan, a faint rumble from within the sunken frame.

Having given us our audience, the Ajahn is swung around again to face the path. The novice slowly nudges him forward. I watch the young Thai's wide lips smile blissfully. He gazes tenderly at his helpless charge, the famous teacher. How much merit will he earn for his *karuna* towards the great monk? The novice is one of those Thais whose sex and age are undeterminable. He could be anywhere from sixteen to fifty. His features are soft and effeminate, a characteristic common among monks, accentuated by their shaven heads. He has pudgy cheeks and a fat neck which bulges at the back. As he steers past us I notice his thick ankles and his flat feet which make no sound as he walks. He reminds me of a young mother fawning over her new-born baby in a pram. The novice with the fan is skinny and tall. He wears glasses and an earnest expression. His lips are pressed together in concentration on his humble task. Actually, the late afternoon air is a little cool, now that the clouds have come up to blot out the sun. He has to fan very slowly or else the Ajahn will catch cold.

The attendant who seated us returns with a plastic sitting mat. He speaks a few words with Ruk in Thai, then brings a plastic tray holding two glasses and a bottle of drinking water. Ruk thanks him while I pour for the two of us. My throat and body are dry. It has been a long walk. We have to return to Pah Nanachat tonight. I drink, surprised by the chill. The water has been refrigerated. The Ajahn comes around to us again. His left eye is partially open. The right opens as well as he approaches. I think they are blue, but they can't be. He is a Thai. I have just spent too long in a *wat* full of nordic *farang*. His gaze seems to fix on me for a moment. Then it flickers to Ruk. I watch intently for some sign of recognition by the master of the monk he named "Laughter." There is none. The eyes begin to wander aimlessly. The twitching right hand has fallen still. He does not even moan. This is a body, I think, a living corpse. The personality—whether ego or inner spirit, whatever it is that gives life—is gone.

It was only illusion to begin with.

Is this freedom from suffering? Certainly there is the chill of emptiness in those wandering eyes. He is detached. A stroke is as effective as *samadhi*-suicide for that. Does the Ajahn also serve as our example? Is he preserved for our edification? Perhaps now he has become the embodiment of the monk's ideal. Jim would criticize his complacency. Wheeled around all day, fed through a tube, dressed and bathed by devotees, he doesn't contribute anything concrete to society…. They will not let him die.

A new group of Thai *bhikkhus*[13] comes and joins us on the grass. Ruk tells me they are on *tudong*[14] from the far south. They have come all this way to meet the holy monk. They wait patiently for him to make his next pass. The novice with the fat neck halts the chair to face the newcomers. After they bow, he begins to turn again to his round but a feeble groan comes from the body in the chair. The novice's eyes widen with joy like a mother's when her baby burbles. He moves the chair back in front of the visitors, letting his charge enjoy their company a minute more. The master's right arm begins to twitch violently. It flops from his lap, dangling loosely beside the chair. The attendant carefully replaces it, tucking the errant limb securely under an orange lap blanket. The Ajahn's focus seems poorer than on the previous round. The eyes wander independently of each other. The visiting monks seem pleased with the interview. They bow again. As the wheelchair swings back to face the path, they stand and return to their van.

Fourth time around, Ruk and I also kneel for our parting bows. These are the most sincere bows I will ever make wearing my *pakhao*[15] robes. I learned much because of this man. His books showed me living wisdom in the Theravada tradition. His skill as a teacher resulted not only in Pah Nanachat, but in fifty-nine other centres dedicated to the Dhamma. His special ability to work with Westerners attracted enough of them for me to be able to experience life in a Thai monastery without having to learn a new and difficult language. He opened all this to me. He is my teacher and I owe much reverence to him. Even if nothing but a shell and symbol remains. With my final bow I pray that this is so, for his sake.

At the front of the bungalow, Ruk finds the senior monk. He asks me to wait on the lawn while they go through details of the visa forms. I stand by the cement pathway and watch the black clouds gathering in the direction of Bung Wai. A monsoon rain is coming our way with the night. Already it is past six. We will walk home in darkness. I feel the blades of grass with my bare feet. A bird flies by, swoops down the hill of the bungalow and over the trees of Pah Pong's jungle. A jagged streak of lightning cuts the black horizon.

Behind me, the wheelchair approaches along the path as the Ajahn rolls through his last few rounds. The novice frown and motions that I should quickly kneel and *wai* before the teacher passes. Ajahn Chah's eyes are open again. They seem to fix on me as he comes close. I read a look from them which cuts to my spine, pulls the muscles in my neck and stomach tight. My skin is suddenly cold. I hold that look, unable to determine whether or not what I see is really there. He passes, leaving me frozen like stone.

I have seen this look once before, in the eyes of an old woman in the examining room of a busy hospital. Her body was failing. Emphysema. Fluid choked her lungs and lack of oxygen was slowly suffocating her mind. Too slowly. She was gradually going insane. The doctor had prodded her naked body and shone a light at her. He wrote on a clipboard and disappeared. She could not speak. Her hand clutched at my shirt like a drowning woman. Her eyes came clear for a moment, pleading me to help. Not like this, not months longer. My eyes darted around the room. But they found nothing sharp. My grandmother's horror possessed me too. In that instant we both realized how long it could take to die.

A crack of thunder releases me. I jerk myself around on the grass to face the black storm, wrenching the muscles in my back. A heavy rain will catch us this night. Good.

## Notes

1. *Ajahn*: (Thai) teacher, guru.
2. *wat*: Thai Buddhist temple or monastery.
3. *peepahs*: (Thai) forest ghosts.
4. *kuties*: plural of *kuti*; (Thai) small one room hut(s) where forest monks live.
5. *sala*: (Thai) main temple of a monastery.
6. *farang*: (Thai) foreign, not Thai, foreigners. Use is both singular and plural. Mildly derogatory.
7. *bot*: (Thai) ordination hall for monks and novices.
8. *samadhi*: (Pali) absorption meditation, "one-pointedness."
9. *pansa*: (Pali) the rains retreat, lasting the three months of monsoon season as determined by the lunar calendar. Monks must not spend a night away from their monastery at this time of year.
10. *Dhamma*, the: (Pali) teachings of the Buddha, the Pali suttas, the doctrine of Buddhism.
11. *dasanas*: (Pali) a sermon about dhamma or the Dhamma.
12. *wai*: (Thai) Buddhist gesture of respect, palms pressed together, hands held up to the face.
13. *bikkhus*: (Pali) literally, devotees (male), monks.
14. *tudong*: (Thai) a monk's pilgrimage from place to place.
15. *pakhao*: (Thai) one who takes the eight precepts and lives in a monastery. In Thailand, usually women.

# PART IV

# Teaching, Limitations, and Marginalization in Suffering

# Chapter 8: The Give-Back of the Giving

*Kelley Aitken*

I'm coming up the stairs from the subway at King station. Less than a meter from the top step sits a tall skinny woman. Hair the colour and texture of straw pokes out from under her floppy deerstalker hat. She's panhandling. I tap her on the shoulder and smile.

"Hey, Bossy Lady!" Jeanie holds her hand to the side of her wide grin and *sotto voce,* adds, "I shouldn't be here."

Jeanie usually lays claim to another corner. She has regular patrons who buy her paintings, swiftly executed swirls of acrylic on canvas board. She tells me it takes her a couple of hours or more to garner the $30 or so it takes to get her through the day. Jeanie's needs are direct and simple: wine-cut-with-water, a nice little steak or chop from the St. Lawrence Market, potatoes, onions, maybe a bit of veg. Lately, I've been extolling the virtues of broccoli.

"You need greens in your diet."

"Okay, Bossy Lady."

The nickname is embarrassingly apt. Jeanie coined it after just one session in the art program at the Adelaide Resource Centre for Women. While the other instructors are overwhelmingly positive in their approach, my teaching style can be characterized by three words:

---

K. Aitken (✉)
Toronto, ON, Canada

© The Author(s) 2019
S. Steel and A. Homeniuk (eds.),
*Suffering and the Intelligence of Love in the Teaching Life,*
https://doi.org/10.1007/978-3-030-05958-3_13

No! Don't! Stop! Jeanie's ability to observe, name and tease me for this tendency in one fell swoop is evidence of a survival instinct honed in the ravines and under the bridges of our fair city. Though housed now in a subsidized apartment, she was living rough when she first came to the program.

"No matter how cold it is," she explained recently, "you never get *inside* the sleeping bag, because you might need to get the hell outta there." One night, she awoke to voices in the parking lot near her bivouac. "Three, four guys—they were coming for me. I threw off my covers, grabbed two empty beer bottles and smashed the ends off them, then went whooping across the parking lot like a crazy lady. They just turned and ran."

Jeanie makes the trek downtown on a daily basis, returning to her old panhandling spot. Does she feel a loss of liberty, I ask? Yes and no, she says. Making a home is hard after years of constant migration within the city limits, carrying only her sleeping roll and clothing. The building has seen violence: a month ago, a woman who lived in an apartment two floors above Jeanie's was killed. But what's really getting to her is the ennui of the other residents. "I keep telling them about this program," she says. "But they won't come."

* * *

What I get from this work—teaching art twice a week at a women's centre—is anchoring. Odd eh? given that it's a program for homeless women, or women whose housing needs are barely met. They live in shelters or in government housing and so, not surprisingly, are territorial (about their stuff and where they want to sit, about how long they've been in the program, about the sink and the coffee urn). If art is essentially a reflection of belonging or identity, then the craving to be involved in artistic practice could be described as a psychic "going home," or "being at home." Certain projects (the less demanding ones that focus on pattern and colour) produce, in the room, a kind of low hum of contentment, a homey feeling.

The Women's Art Afternoon is a community art program facilitated by Toronto's Regent Park Community Health Centre. It is housed in the Adelaide Resource Centre for Women, an un-bedded shelter that offers a variety of day programs and services for women experiencing long term poverty. The program provides a safe and inclusive environment where women can participate in creative expression.

I've been teaching there since 2001. Along with my colleague Camille Winchester, I co-teach a smaller more independent group with dedicated enrolment on Mondays, and on Thursdays I alternate every three weeks with another instructor for the larger drop-in program. The instructors come up with the projects, many of which build individual components into a collaborative piece. We offer instruction in acrylic and watercolour painting; drawing using a variety of media and techniques; collage and assemblage; printmaking; encaustic; hand-building in clay; mosaic; plasticine animation, etc. On Thursdays, I am joined by a team: three social workers, students on placement and, occasionally, volunteers. We have a decent budget for supplies. Every week a few of the women earn honorariums by assisting with set up and clean up. (Jeanie, for example, plunges the perpetually clogged sink.)

Some of my recent projects have involved a slightly theatrical approach: mask- and hat- making using recycled papers, a communal skirt sewn together from individually designed panels, which we stepped into and sort of shuffle-danced in. Another instructor is an actor/artist/therapist who begins the class with movement: stretches and vocalizations. Given what some of the women can *say* to us and each other, the fact that this makes them shy is rather sweet. Movement makes us notice each other fully, head to toe, front to back—uncertainty gives way to smiles. In life-drawing sessions the women have taken turns posing for one another.

I get a sense of myself offering something real, and that has less to do with art—although that's the reason we're all there in the same place, with me giving my dorky little demonstrations—than with showing up as myself. Those women don't cooperate, at least not in that middle of the road, middle-class way; they demand and beg and grab; they compete for things, ask for "presents" and want things outright: my time, supplies, praise, to sell their work. This certainty and directness saves a lot of time.

Perhaps in a setting like that I enjoy a certain paradox: I can stretch myself into a more honest shape while enjoying the theatricality. It's a big room; I have to speak in a loud voice, telling jokes and little anecdotes to snag and keep their attention, if only for the few minutes of my demonstrations, and inserted throughout the class. But in that moment, I am also establishing something I think of as central to teaching. I'm saying to them: we're equals. Of course, in many ways, we're not equal: I get paid and they don't; I have art training and they don't; and I am more or less free of mental health issues, at least the permanently disabling kind.

Yet the women want what's on offer here and are both humble and brash about what they make. That's the genius of the program: creativity can be paradoxically a blissful melting pot and an opportunity for individuals to shine. The mechanics are in place; staff members provide the materials, the necessary instruction, the all-important coffee and tea, and the ongoing support. But the women provide their willingness, that hum of attention and concentration, which is communal permission, energy, and release. Each woman takes what she needs, engages, and produces, and her artwork says to her: you exist; this reflects you; your feelings are real.

These women have experienced deprivation, addiction, emotional, physical and sexual abuse. They have dissociating tendencies, mental health concerns, and developmental delays. It's hard for a lot of them to learn new skills. And because of that, I've had to develop a kind of full-on body involvement in my teaching: lots of demonstration followed by one-on-one attention. Both of those incorporate cajoling; teasing; encouragement; acting out a process; and finally, giving up what I think of as a good result and going with the flow.

Sometimes it's calm. Sometimes, it's not. Mental health is a pendulum; no one is exempt, and rarely is our position stationary. Much has been written about the proximity of madness and intense creativity, probably too much. But I am getting somewhere with this, so bear with me. It's not just that "the gloves are off" with this group; some of the women have outbursts, spark off each other in anger or frustration, speak out of turn, and out of line. In the more extreme ends of their schizophrenic spectrum, the fact that some women get there at all is an achievement. But when they're experiencing equilibrium—man, oh man (woman, oh woman!)—I'd kill to draw like that, to *see* like that, so freely, without concern for accuracy, good taste, or "artfulness." And because they're not afraid, their slaps and blobs of paint are fearless; their weird illustrator or robot-y figures and mask-like faces are haunting; their palettes are surprising; their marks are bold and vigorous; their compositions are exquisite. It's so true to who they are; the channel to the psyche is wide open and pumping. Marla, another participant said, and I paraphrase, "If the choice is between medication and art, I'll choose art."

Forced by circumstances to compete for space, these women are by turns exhibitionist and larger than life, or capable of creating a force-field around themselves and their work. They mug for my camera; they display their work with pride; they give me back far more than the ideas and materials I brought into the room.

How does this benefit my practice? That begs the question; what is my practice? Not just the in-studio creation, but the way I am in the world. Teaching is a communicative art. It's a way to establish intimacy, community; it's an acceptable and widely-used form of therapy. Teaching is service, and it's an act of engagement. Like fiction writing, it touches on what Amos Oz refers to as "a moral incept,"[1] curiosity about others, imagining what it's like to be in that skin, that body, that life.

\* \* \*

Some years have passed since I wrote this essay. In 2011, after ten years, I left my twice weekly job at the Adelaide Centre. I felt I was getting repetitive and cranky, and the women deserved better. We are all replaceable, and the younger women who took over the job brought new energy, projects, and insight to that amazing, difficult, inspiring, and resilient community.

Living on the streets or in perpetual poverty take its toll. A number of the women have died, including, I am sad to say, Jeannie, who was so full of life.

It was a formative experience for me as a teacher. I teach now at the Art Gallery of Ontario, and occasionally at the Aga Khan Museum where I am meeting a new population and working with a fabulous collection of Islamic art. In these galleries, my students are often retired professionals, people for whom creativity can finally be a focus. A great many of them are teachers. But nothing will ever have quite the same impact as that decade at the Women's Art Program. Why?

Sean has asked me to address the notion of suffering in teaching. This may seem like an easy out, a liberal lefty's refrain: I got out of it at least as much as I gave. The minute the women arrived I had to be on my toes. This was in-your-face teaching; in-your-face interactions; crazy ladies; honesty; anger; distrust; remembering to ask myself, when one or more of the women said or did something that was triggering: "Whose need is greater?" And I didn't always do that; I did not always behave with the maturity that the women were entitled to expect or that I expected from myself. I definitely saw suffering and its long-term effects. I saw women whose lives were not going to get a lot better. I saw women whose sexuality left them marooned between genders because they lacked the supportive frameworks, or upbringing, or financial means to get all the way across that divide. Issues of mental health grind people down, and there are memories that people cannot rise above or forgive, or even get around. When you work in the shelter system, you observe all of that and alongside it, a kind of fatigued tirelessness on the part of devoted social workers; and over it all you feel the weight of expectation in the bureaucracy of our so-called civilized society.

One way that I do suffer, now, as a teacher and perhaps always have, is in not getting to my own work, not applying the guidance I give to others to myself in terms of my own drawing, painting, and writing. When I don't address this, I can resent my students, and I become impatient with those individuals who have viable learning blocks, or who require too much reassurance.

But teaching is a backbone too. In times of personal hardship, it has afforded me structure, security, and a chance, even for a few hours, to put my own suffering aside. Teaching allows me to leave myself at the door, to *act* as door, window, or mirror so that a student can find inspiration, or develop capacity. And that has allowed me to discover things about the observed world that I did not know I knew. This is the excitement of teaching others how to look and how to see. Exchanges with many of my students have been a source of inspiration. For myself, I need to establish the balance between outward and inward. The teacher needs to teach herself.

## Note

1. Amos Oz, interview with Eleanor Wachtel, *Writers and Company*, CBC Radio, September 19, 2010. http://www.cbc.ca/player/play/1595225735.

## Reference

Oz, Amos. Interview with Eleanor Wachtel. *Writers and Company*. CBC Radio. September 19, 2010.

# Chapter 9: Teaching Tiny Tim from My Tiny Tim Closet—A Personal Essay

*Dorothy Ellen Palmer*

In my three decades of teaching, I never taught a book with a disabled hero.

I never taught a book about a disabled woman.

As an English and Drama teacher, I taught plenty of books and plays with disabled villains, all of them male, all of them damaged, and all of them able to damage me if I let them.

As teachers of literature, we work hard to find books that represent our diverse students. No one ever talks about the fact that diverse teachers suffer the same erasure and silencing. We spend our entire professional lives teaching a curriculum that misrepresents and excludes us. We never see our authentic selves in what we teach. Rather than face that exclusion, I spent my career pretending not to be disabled. Now that I'm retired, I realize my complicity in my own oppression. I reproduced in my students the very same ableist privilege that kept me silent.

Can we teach beyond the stereotype of Tiny Tim? I never managed to do so.

---

D. E. Palmer (✉)
Burlington, ON, Canada

After an Honours B.A. at the University of Western Ontario, and teacher training in the new "Multicultural Module" at Simon Fraser University, I began teaching in 1983. My first job: teaching Grade Five in La Crete, a Mennonite colony on the Alberta side of the N.W.T. border. I also taught in a four-room school house in Olds, Alberta, home of holocaust denier Jim Keegstra, and an Adult learning center in Calgary next to a prison where some students arrived escorted and in chains. When I moved back to Ontario, I taught in two older high schools, and for the last fifteen years of my career, in a brand new highly diverse high school in Pickering.

For all these years, I hid in the disabled closet. I doped and denied my pain. However else we define it. teaching excellence contains one unalterable criteria: we must be indefatigably able-bodied. And cheerful. Don't forget cheerful. When the childhood corrective surgery of the birth defects in my feet began to fail, when arthritis set in, when my invisible disability became visible and I began to need a crutch, I lied. I said it was only temporary. Rather than become a teacher with a walker, because I had never seen a teacher with a walker and was in too much pain to be the first of my kind, I retired.

So many other closets got proudly thrown open during my career, but not mine.

When I began teaching in 1983, there were no openly gay or lesbian teachers. Coming out would have cost them their jobs. Over time, we welcomed gay and lesbian department heads, elected union reps, administrators, and consultants. Schools had openly dating gay and lesbian couples. I attended the wedding of two lesbian kindergarten teachers, held in their school library.

Similarly, as a beginning teacher, I had no openly gay or lesbian students. Coming out would have cost them their teeth. In the 1990s, students began coming out in Grade Thirteen. By 2008, when I retired, many were out by Grade Nine. We had joint staff and student Pride Committees.

When I began teaching, school leadership from student council to administration, was all-white and all male. The only employees of colour were custodians. My career saw initiatives such as STAR: Students and Teachers Against Racism and students of colour as student council presidents. At retirement, half my colleagues were women. We had a black woman principal. And a quarter of my colleagues were teachers of colour, a change still evolving.

But my closet stayed closed. No disabled liberation movement ever developed.

People with disabilities are twenty percent of the planet, but the able-bodied ruled every aspect of my workplace for my entire career. I had no openly disabled colleagues. Once they were off probation, some colleagues privately divulged invisible disabilities, but begged me not to tell anyone. As union Branch President, I saw our contractual long-term disability clauses improve, but our entire union mind set was to assist teachers who became disabled mid-career. And by "assist," we meant to fairly pension them out of teaching on long-term disability. There were no initiatives to hire disabled teachers into teaching. We had no staff with mobility devices, none in wheelchairs. In a confluence of reasons, the inaccessibility of school buildings and teacher training, and the prejudices of teaching hiring, the change that blossomed in other marginalized communities never took root. The domination of athletic boys and girls that began on the playground, replicated itself in high school, and normalized the continued power and privilege of the able-bodied to run high schools.

My disabled students, especially neuro-divergent students, sought out the alternate identities of tech and nerd culture. They found self-esteem excelling at programming and gaming, by joining a fandom, or Live Action Role Play: L.A.R.P. In my theatre, I created another refuge: the only two-year, two-credit, improv program in Canada. Touring both elementary and high schools, my improv students offered interactive workshops to combat racism, homophobia, sexual harassment, and bullying. Thanks to every-Friday lunchtime shows, my improvisors gained the status of football stars. We even had a winning team. My improv teams advanced to the national level of The Canadian Improv games.

My career paralleled the rise of male stand-up comics to celebrity status. Eddie Murphy, Robin Williams, and Scarborough's own Mike Myers, made it entirely permissible for boys to take improv. The girls had to fight the boys for air time, but today we have a whole generation of comics like Tina Fey, Samantha Bee, and Kate McKinnon, who teach all my students what few of us believed when I began teaching: Yes, girls are funny, too.

But did any of this newly expanded equity apply to my disabled students?

No, it did not. Time passed and left them where the world saw them. In stasis.

When I began teaching, the only disabled comic I'd ever seen on TV was Geri Jewell. She was the first comic with cerebral palsy, the first disabled actor period, to have a role in a prime-time series: *The Facts of Life*. But it ran from 1980 to 1984. None of my recent students had heard of her. Every year, when I asked my classes to name another disabled comic, poet, playwright, or writer, none of them ever could. And it wasn't their fault.

Curriculum representing other diverse communities evolved with the times. Publishers and librarians made sincere efforts to include women authors, and culturally diverse stories. In my English classroom, I received class sets of *The Colour Purple* and *The Handmaid's Tale*. For independent studies, I had an ever-increasing number of culturally diverse books to recommend to all my students. The buzz word of the day, *multicultural education*, championed the diversity of geography, language, race, colour, and culture. Although people with disabilities are truly intersectional, although we come from every other marginalized group, we remained invisible.

I want to make it incandescently clear that teachers are not to blame for this.

You can't teach books about disabled lives if none are published.

You can't buy any new books, without a budget. We barely had funds to repair old books, let alone the purchase of new ones. Getting new diverse books into Canadian high schools requires a dedicated, government-checked budget, funds a principal can't siphon off to the football team. To get new books, my colleagues and I pulled out our purses. On my own dime, I became the first Canadian high school teacher to stage Ntozake Shange's Tony nominated play, *For Coloured Girls Who Have Considered Suicide/When the Rainbow is Enough*. Learning from that cast of seven amazing young black women became the best experience of my career.

Here's how I sum it up now that I'm done: although I led and welcomed change, I never got it for myself. I went my whole life, a full half a century as student and teacher, longing for books with people who looked like me. Longing to teach them. Longing to read them. To my students, to my children, and for myself. If I'd had books with disabled protagonists, perhaps I could have gained the courage to leave my closet. Instead, the all-pervasive ableism of those books I did have to teach kept my closet shut with the death grip of Hodor, the brave disabled giant from *Game of Thrones* who died holding his door closed.

In the high school curriculum, disability has no presence except a negative one.

I could not counter the fairy tale of free-floating bile, all the implicit and explicit messages that spread the first lie of ableism: that beautiful people are deserving and good, and conversely, that disabled characters are ugly and crippled at heart. Every teaching day, I had to force feed my twenty-first century students with the poison of medieval eugenics, with the lies that led to Hitler's disabled cleansing. With a hidden breaking heart, I explained that in "great" works of literature a damaged body was predisposed, if not predetermined, to harbor a monstrous soul. Maligning my community and myself, I told my students a disabled body might house a brilliant evil mind, but never a brilliant mind and a kind human heart. Shakespeare enshrined the evil cripple of Richard III. From Long-John Silver to Captain Hook, amputation of the body decreed an amputation of empathy. Disability fueled Frankenstein hate, an envy that disfigured monsters inevitably took out on the innocent world. "A broken body," I can hear myself saying, "dictates a broken moral compass and the moral depravity of Doctor Strangelove."

When we discussed *The Elephant Man*, my students parroted back the first rule of inspiration porn: that it makes the able-bodied feel good about themselves to notice disabled people doing something normal. My students uniformly informed me that Joseph Merrick was gross, but was also a hero because he was nice to people. I had to wait decades to see my first authentically kind disabled genius in film: Professor Charles Xavier of *X-Men*. Bless him.

And speaking of inspiration porn, few of my students had read Dicken's *A Christmas Carol*, but from Disney, to Jim Carrey, to the Muppets, they all knew who Tiny Tim was and what he stood for. They accepted his angelic death without question. Just as they equally accepted that the first boy to die in *Lord of the Flies* was the one with the mulberry birthmark. Both deaths make perfect sense in the ableist hierarchy we all absorb from childhood. Be a good little Tiny Tim and we'll pat you on your inspiring head until you die. Speak up, try and name the beast, complain or criticize, and we'll kill you. We won't even bother to learn your name.

Trying to counter the brainwashing my students and I had suffered since childhood, was overwhelming and exhausting. Even on TV, most disabled characters were men, and to quote the important insight of Lady Gaga, none of them "were born that way." Crippled later in life, by injury, accident, or war, they typically suffer not just a fall from grace, but a fall from athletic over-achieving able-bodied grace. I loved Raymond Burr, the Perry Mason of my childhood, in the role of a wheelchair detective, but *Ironside* embodies the one permissible disabled TV narrative. After being shot in the line of duty, he's *grateful* to be a consultant. He lives in San Francisco, but we never see him struggling to push his manual wheelchair up hills or being carried over curbs and up flights of stairs. His story is the one able-bodied viewers want to see: one that says disability is all a matter of *attitude*. Robert T. Ironside literally has iron sides, and a matching iron will to prove the loss of mobility is no loss at all. He not only copes, he excels, the implicit message being that it is formerly able-bodied people who have the grit to do disability right. *They* get to be our role models. *They* get to "triumph over disability," to teach all of us disabled from birth how to stop complaining and jump on the inspiration porn bandwagon.

In both literature and media, the disabled "role models" offered in high schools are frequently veterans. After proving their ultra-able-bodied masculinity as soldiers, their "demotion" to the ranks of the disabled reduces them to symbols of the damage of war. They don't live authentic disabled lives; they wage a second personal war to defeat their disability. In *Forrest Gump*, not only does Forrest shed his braces, the bitter Lt. Dan learns to walk again on prosthetics, and having battled back to the able-bodied world, also triumphs over PTSD. James Cameron's *Avatar*, in all its award-winning cinematic glory, says only one thing to me: A disabled veteran's life isn't worth living. It's better to leave that body behind for a drug-induced fantasy, to hang out with sexy, swinging blue aliens. This is the same underlying message as the recent disabled snuff film, *Me Before You*, which in the guise of romance asserts that disabled people will never live full, complete lives, and thus should logically choose to kill themselves.

Thank goodness comics entered the twenty-first century long before literature or TV.

That's where I found a plethora of mid-twentieth century disabled heroes, even if they are also often superhuman. As early as 1941, Dr. Charles Mc Nider became Dr. Midnight. Blinded by a hand grenade, he developed the power to see in the dark. Captain Marvel Jr. lived a double life as crippled newsboy, Freddy Freeman. In the 1960s Marvel version, disabled Dr. Donald Blake transformed into the mighty Thor. When teenage Matt Murdock saves a blind man from being hit by a truck, he becomes Daredevil, whose blindness is "mutagenically heightened" by the truck's radioactive waste. And comic books gave us our first disabled women heroes: Oracle, a wheel chair computer geek, and Silhouette, paralyzed in her own body, but with superpower martial arts skills. Although these disabilities do little more than counterpoint superpowers and perpetuate the notion that disabled people long for healing and escape, comic books did something no other media did at the time: They saw us. They made us visible.

It wasn't until 1989 that I saw a physically disabled protagonist who was, "born that way." Daniel Day Lewis in *My Left Foot*, won what I saw at the time as a much-deserved Academy Award playing Christy Brown, a real-life Irish writer and painter with cerebral palsy. Like my feet, his were different one from the other. Thrilled to see another physically disabled writer on screen, it never occurred to me that a disabled actor could play a disabled man. In the 1980s, it never occurred to anyone that *not* seeing disabled people acting in their own roles and performing in their own bodies, might be one of the things that kept us in the closet.

And we're still seeing imposters. Even in 2017, some 95% of disabled characters in film and TV are played by able-bodied actors. In some cases, such as Eddie Redmayne's portrayal of Stephen Hawking, an able-bodied actor is needed to play able-bodied years. But in many cases, there is no excuse. Just as hiring white actors to play Asian or Black roles is deservedly under fire, it's long past time to see disabled actors. Teachers need them. Students need them. As much as I loved Artie on *Glee*, he is yet another able-bodied person kindly teaching us how to handle our disabilities. After the rousing finale, we all knew Kevin McHale got up and walked off set.

It wasn't until I had retired from teaching improv that I met my first funny disabled characters: the memory-impaired Dory in *Finding Dory*, and the Viking horde in the *How to Train your Dragon* movies. These Hairy Hooligans warriors rewrite stereotypes. Toothless the Dragon flies with a mended wing that he uses to his advantage. He's a role model for his nerdy young rider, unlikely Viking Prince Hiccup Horrendous Haddock III, when he gets lamed by losing his foot in battle. And I adore Gobber the Belch who has lost both an arm and leg to dragon fighting. He is most certainly the first disabled Viking dragon hunter to come out of the closet as openly gay.

But while I was a teacher, the lack of disabled role models, the lack of any discussion at all about disability, meant that I held the door of my closet shut against both my students and my colleagues. I stood at the blackboard all day, and in the theatre all night. Only slowly, and in bits and pieces, did I admit anything to my colleagues about why I had a "handicapped parking permit." If all the smart women who taught with me wondered why a woman who quilted, who loved fabric and colour, showed up each day in little boy's running shoes, they never asked me about it. I guess I played my role too well. They saw it only as what I'd said it was for years: my refusal to look like a Barbie doll, my personal feminist fashion statement.

They never knew I couldn't wear any other kind of shoes.

They never knew shoes tore at my scars and filled with blood.

Wear a costume long enough and it isn't one, it's your wardrobe. It becomes what people see and expect to see. And what they never question. Only my Harry Potter loving daughter saw it for what it was: My cloak of invisibility. One I wore while I reached out to every marginalized community but my own. One that kept me from reaching out to my own.

The closest I ever came to coming out of my disabled closet was in improv class.

I worked hard to help my students understand that victim humor was cheap, that we could be funny without it. I forbade second language accents, racist and sexist "jokes." I took a whole period to discuss why Apu on *The Simpsons* wasn't funny. Hardest to convince were the funniest white boys in the class for whom racial ridicule was a staple of their comedic success. It took no convincing at all for my black and brown students, who taught the class on this subject much better than I ever could. Together, we reached for a more complex humour, used humour to explore beyond comedy. Together, we built a safe laboratory to test drive the choices in our lives. And we honoured Robin Williams, using humour to face every lonely darkness.

Except my own. I had no words for it yet.

The very language of teaching is the language of ableism. Of your standing in the class. Of coming first, or last. Of winners and losers. Field trips and field days. Pep rallies for the big game where our boys slaughter the enemy. Seizing the brass ring, or failing to make your mark.

Teaching is ableist to its very core; it praises "a healthy mind" in "a healthy body."

It behaves at every moment as if achieving both is nothing but a matter of will.

The word *ableism* didn't come into my vocabulary until after I retired. Without my own language, I did what I could. I insisted that my students keep their use of slapstick to a minimum, for safety reasons. I didn't understand then what I see so clearly now: that it is entirely ableist to laugh at tripping and falling, to see an able-bodied person's temporary "humiliation" and "demotion to incapacitation" as funny. When my students did so, I felt sick, but told myself that was my problem, not the problem.

Because when I did try to stick up for myself, I didn't get taken seriously.

I convinced hundreds of teens to stop saying, "That's so gay!" but I had trouble convincing anyone to stop saying, "That's so lame!" Able-bodied teen gatekeepers watched me limp and told me *lame* wasn't an insult. They told me, and I repeat for emphasis, these smug, healthy, able-bodied children told me, that *lame* meant what it means to all my otherwise politically-correct well-educated friends when they so casually use it: *Wrong. Inadequate. A pathetic second best. Half-hearted, fake. Lazy and laughable. Invalid.*

Yep, that's me. I'm so lame. I let them steal the word that is me.

I let the world warp the truth of my body, let others use the word for my body, to smear me as inferior. For years, when I challenged able-bodied colleagues about their use of the word *lame*, after two seconds of reflection they apologized, then used it again the next day.

If I learned anything from my years of doing anti-sexist, anti-racist, anti-homophobic work as a high school teacher, it's this: the foundation of any privilege is *not having to see it*, being able to assume that your world view is universal, normal, and always right. Able-bodied privilege works the same way. It gets away with claiming a difference between intent and impact. My students and friends don't intend to sound like assholes when they call something lame, but the impact of their words is assholian. When I asked one of my oldest colleagues to at least stop saying "that's so lame" in front of me, they said: "Come on, Dorothy. You may have a disability, I acknowledge that. But, hey, that disability doesn't have you!"

Utter crap. My disability has me dead to rights. It has had me all along.

I only never talked about it because I internalized the shame. And, ironically, I never talked about my suffering precisely because disability activists, who reject the medical model of disability and embrace the social model, totally reject any word that even sounds like *suffer*. We don't "suffer" as disabled people. We live full authentic lives. We are not pitiable. Unfortunately, this left me without words for suffering, let alone words to name the ways I suffered.

Nobody knew that silencing better than my disabled students, the one marginalized group of that to this day I wish I'd served better. My last school, built in 1992 to new accessibility standards, was the first, and then the only, high school in my district to boast the stairless accessibility of ramps and an elevator. Disabled students from all over the district were bussed in. Sometimes, but only in private, I pried my closet door open just enough for them to peek in. Sometimes, I confided my own years on crutches and in a wheel chair. How their eyes widened at the unthinkable notion that a teacher could be disabled. They'd never seen such a creature. I tried to encourage my disabled students with a love for Drama to audition for school plays and try out for the improv team. I wasn't surprised when they did neither.

I was no hero. I followed the "I see no disability," approach of my teaching colleagues. Full of hand-picked young teachers, my school held endless workshops and initiatives on every other social justice topic, but no one championed "the wheelchair kids." Defining them by their chair, kept them at a distance, as if they were an alien Borg sub-species. I don't know if other teachers ever saw what I did: that other than the able-bodied "buddies" assigned to them by the guidance office for the first week of Grade Nine, the wheelchair kids had no able-bodied friends. They studied alone. They ate alone. While teachers would never suggest that students of colour "segregated themselves" in the cafeteria, that same phrasing went unchallenged for our disabled students. Their "self-exclusion" remained unaddressed and unchallenged.

Politically-progressive and caring teachers battling every other kind of "ism," saw no "ism" to fight.

Instead, I sometimes saw "pity marks." And the placating of parents. I want to stress that the vast majority of parents of disabled students are like all parents: earnest and learning. But the era of Participation Awards affected us all. Perhaps some parents were exhausted from fighting doctors, agencies, and decades of other teachers. Perhaps they overcompensated to cover their truly justified concerns for their child's future. Whatever the reasons, on parents' night, some insisted, all-too-often in front of their child, that their Judy or Jamal may be *physically* disabled, but was *mentally* a genius. You either gave their kid an A, or you got phone calls, and threats to escalate to a superintendent, until you did so. This hyper-vigilant minority only perpetuated a wariness, strengthened the existing division between disabled student and able-bodied teacher.

Of course, many teachers built personal relationships with individual disabled students. But in all my years of teaching, no one ever saw them as a collective. No one ever reached out to them collectively. No one ever encouraged them to see themselves that way, to use their combined voices to speak up, and out, about their lives. Everyone, including me, smiled at them in the hall, then turned our backs and left the wheelchair kids alone to fend for themselves.

This is the first time I've ever admitted this failure, still painful years later.

I still struggle to explain why I couldn't do better. I think I had lived too much of my life being able to pass in the walking world. I'd worked for and benefited from my years of able-bodied privilege. I couldn't give it up. Without role models, without curriculum, without allies, without language, I couldn't fight alone. I couldn't come out of my own closet.

Today, are there more disabled teachers in schools? Are there novels with disabled heroes that all students read? I doubt it. Are there initiatives to hear, and really listen to, the voices of disabled students? I don't know. I do know today's teachers will still have to hunt down disability-positive curriculum. They will still have to address their own internalized ableism.

If I were still teaching, I'd like to think I could do Tiny Tim differently.

But the more important question is this: What will new teachers do now?

# Chapter 10: Making Space—It's Okay to Clear Time for Yourself

*Jenna Butler*

There's an old adage in craftsmanship: *Measure twice, cut once.* Quite simply, it means that if you don't want to keep buying materials until the cows come home, take the measure of your project carefully, size it up well and in good time, and then act. Like so many other bits and pieces of learning from the world outside the classroom, it fits well for what we're doing when we step up in front of a class. This adage holds true for everything from how to deal with problem students (bite back your initial retort, count to ten, and then let your calmer self through) to how we approach self-care as educators.

Self-care is one of those terms that's bandied about a lot in the teaching profession, but when it comes to actual practice, let's face it: we pretty much all fall short. It's one thing to think, over the course of the summer, *I'm going to book myself a yoga course three nights a week during the school year, and hey, I've always wanted to try Pilates, and what*

---

J. Butler (✉)
Red Deer College, Red Deer, AB, Canada
e-mail: jenna.butler@rdc.ab.ca

© The Author(s) 2019
S. Steel and A. Homeniuk (eds.),
*Suffering and the Intelligence of Love in the Teaching Life,*
https://doi.org/10.1007/978-3-030-05958-3_15

*about a morning swim on Fridays? I could do that. Plus, the boss wants me to supervise the Chess Club, which is totally manageable...* It's something completely else to look at yourself in the mirror in mid-November, when the bags under your eyes are coming up plain, and realize, *Hey, I need to make some time for myself. I need to rest right now before I crash.*

*Before* is the key. Measure twice, cut once. Catch yourself before your energy is gone. Learn to suss out when you're in free fall and do whatever you need to do to get yourself back on your feet.

I'm what some in the post-secondary business call an "academhick," and that's part of the reason you'll see me reaching outside the ivory tower for advice on how to live in the world. When I'm not in my classroom, I run an off-grid organic farm with my husband in northern Alberta, a place we built together from the ground up. That's the place I turn to on a weekly basis during the school year to help take the measure of my own energy—what I have to give, and what I need to build back up for myself. It's the place where I can most clearly find myself amidst the many demands of teaching.

As educators, when we enter the school building, we tend to lose our sense of self. It's a no-brainer: when you're responsible for the learning of young people, and you're also often a go-to life counselor, your boundaries blur. You don't realize how much energy you're giving, day in and day out, until your reserves run dry. I've watched teachers hit bottom, and I've come perilously close myself. It's not something people talk openly about in education, and that needs to change. We are caretakers at our cores. We need to create the language for talking about self-care as educators, *and we need to learn to follow through*. I've watched fellow teachers self-medicate with alcohol, Percocet, Prozac, Xanax, Clonazepam; you name it, they tried it to reduce the anxiety and fear of hitting bottom. I've gone through those periods of intense fear myself, times when I've been so tired and so depleted that the thought of getting up in front of a single roomful of new students, let alone my standard yearly complement of 350 college kids, has made me want to crawl back into bed and cry.

So the focal point is this: *measure twice*. When something else lands on your plate in late October, just as the first half of the year is hitting its stride, really listen to yourself and think, *Can I truly manage this one additional thing?* If the answer is no, learn to say no, clearly and with strength. This is true even when you're starting out in your teaching career. If you can learn early on to sense when you're getting overburdened, you can catch yourself before you get to the point of crashing. Don't worry that your department head or your administration won't respect you if you sit down with them and explain that you can't take on this additional assignment right now. Truly, it's going to be a lot worse for you and for everyone around you if you're in a puddle of tears every morning. Presenting your boundaries to others helps to make them more concrete for yourself.

I mentioned that term *academhick* earlier, a subversive title taken up by professors who are also farmers. That's a role I've come to over time, after over a decade of teaching at the high school, college, and university levels. When I started out as a teacher, I wanted to do everything—everything that was asked of me, everything I could dream up. I wanted to create thrilling classes for my students. I wanted to achieve a permanent job. I thought, surely if I ran myself into the ground trying, I would attain all these things.

What I did do was fry myself right out. In my final year of teaching high school, I had just turned 26. I was in the last year of probationary work before getting my permanent contract, and I was looking good for a solid position with the public school board. I was teaching full-time English Literature, in addition to being the AP English program designer and sole instructor for the school, and I was also the Department Head of English and Fine Arts. Finally, I was completing my Ph.D. at an overseas university, flying back and forth between England and Canada a few times a year to work with my supervisors and face evaluation by committee.

In short, I was seriously running on empty.

What I should have said back then was *no*. *No*, I don't know enough yet as a teacher to be made the department head, let alone the head of two departments. *No*, I can't teach all the AP English by myself. *Yes*, I am incredibly flattered by your faith in me, but I need to learn my way into all these roles to do them right. Can I mentor with someone else for a year first? Can I co-teach until I know what I'm doing? Can I work ¾ time until I finish my Ph.D.?

I burnt out hard and left high school that June, having just received my permanent contract. I needed time off to rest and heal, to recalibrate for a better journey ahead, and to finish my Ph.D., which I had decided to follow through with. My farm became the way of taking the measure of my own energy. My husband and I (he's also a teacher) began the farm together with nothing more than one axe, ours summers off from teaching, and 160 acres of northern bush. Our dream was to build a home where we could live a life of our own pacing, somewhere completely outside the strict timing of the school day.

The farm has taught me everything I'm bringing to you now. It's taught me how slowing down completely feels. We work *hard* out there on the land, but it's a different kind of work: I work with my hands, letting my teaching self rest when needed, and that reminds me that I'm not just a brain up in front of a classroom. I'm a whole person. At the farm, I have to carefully gauge my energy in every physical task, lest I become a danger to myself or others. There's no way I can be tired and haul out the chainsaw. That's a recipe for disaster.

Yes, our farm is a lot of work, but it's productive work. When I'm on the land, I'm helping to grow the food we'll eat for the rest of the year, frozen, dried, or canned. I'm splitting the wood that will heat our cabin. And our farm is the place where, as a writer, I have time in the evenings to return to my own work. In short, it's a way of life that fills my tank.

The farm has taught me to turn inward when I'm about to accept any task and say, *Can I really take this on now and do a good job, or am I too tired? Will it go well, and will it be safe?* If I answer myself honestly and the response is *no*, I turn down the work. Even if it's a great opportunity, I've learned that having energy for my own life and goals, plus energy to bring to my students each day, is more important. Having reached the crash point, I never want to go there again.

If you're starting out on your teaching journey, I want to say two things to you. First, good on you. Teaching isn't a profession for everyone. You have to love bringing energy to your students to get them fired up about learning, and mediating the energy you find already there in the classroom each day. Ultimately, the energy you go into your classroom with will dictate whether you and your students have an awesome day or an awful one.

Second, be good to yourself. Learn to take the measure of what you have to offer. Don't beat yourself up if you need to back down from tasks or opportunities in favour of resting and filling up your own tank. Remember that the more balanced you are, the better teacher you'll be. And don't be afraid to talk about self-care. Your students are looking to you for a lot more than instruction about World War II or fractions or Shakespeare. They're looking to you to start learning how to *be* in the world. If you can show them that taking care of yourself is a positive thing, you're going to teach them so much about self-respect.

It's a balancing act, but it's worth it.

You know this. That's why you're here.

PART V

# Suffering Spiritual Tensions and the Pursuit of Wisdom in Teaching

# Importance

## *Keith Inman*

Sorry for the delay in answering
your kind e-mail
and its raucous follow-up when you
didn't get an immediate response.

I was up north with family
getting away from 'it all.' Up
16 cross-over lanes of weaving drivers late
for funerals. But we made it,
head chefs at a single grill; boaters
stuck on unmarked rocks, our prop
spitting metal.
We showed the children how to fish
from the dock instead,

wild hooks in the air.

And learned the Applied Science
of bandaids, sandfly rashes, stubbed

cottage-carpet-toe, red-thumb-throb
of open deck boards, the fiery depth
of cloud-shoal skies bleeding into night.

I did reply on the open web,
wind-tussled trees, dark paths of knurled
roots alive with borealis stars.
I hope you got that one.

The rest of the week was looking
after the constant
turning, tumbling questions of a five year old
climbed on my back
as we lay on the grass feeding peanuts
to a chipmunk in her hand

inches above the ground.

# Chapter 11: A Teacher's Night Song

*Sean Steel*

Nietzsche's ability to help us understand our lives in relation to wisdom's pursuit has long interested me.[1] In this chapter, I explore the "Night Song" from Friedrich Nietzsche's *Thus Spake Zarathustra* for the insights it offers readers concerning the spiritual yearnings that constitute the contemplative foundations of the teaching life. Particular attention is given to Nietzsche's purposeful inversions of "light" and "darkness" imagery in the poem as these relate to the suffering of subtle, psychic tensions. Having elucidated how Nietzsche's understanding of psychic tensions is related to active willing and passive receptivity, my analysis focuses upon the manner in which teachers' obligations towards students create a learning atmosphere that has certain deleterious effects upon any great hopes of nourishing the precious spirit of wisdom-seeking that ought to underlie all true teaching as a "way of life." We begin with a brief quotation from the passage under study:

---

S. Steel (✉)
Calgary Board of Education, Calgary, AB, Canada

© The Author(s) 2019
S. Steel and A. Homeniuk (eds.),
*Suffering and the Intelligence of Love in the Teaching Life*,
https://doi.org/10.1007/978-3-030-05958-3_17

> Night has come; now all fountains speak more loudly. And my soul too is a fountain.
> Night has come; only now all the songs of lovers awaken. And my soul too is the song of a lover.
> Something unstilled, unstillable is within me; it wants to be voiced. A craving for love is within me; it speaks the language of love.
> Light am I; ah, that I were night! But this is my loneliness that I am girt with light. Ah, that I were dark and nocturnal! How I would suck at the breasts of light! And even you would I bless, you little sparkling stars and glow worms up there, and be overjoyed with your gifts of light.[2]

Imagery of light and darkness is prominent in our ordinary articulations of suffering. Darkness is typically associated with pain, confusion, hopelessness, and meaninglessness. Light, by stark contrast, tends to suggest an awakening of insight, hopefulness, the awareness of meaning, and the cessation of suffering. Moreover, whereas darkness is to be disparaged and avoided at all costs, light is something to be sought out and cultivated. This is the typical manner in which we use the metaphors of light and darkness to speak about not only suffering and experience, but also education.

However, these binary oppositional meanings do not account for all the rich ways in which human beings use the imagery of light and darkness. In this short reflection, I want to explore with you the inversion of this dichotomy, for there is, in fact, a kind of attractive and *educational* darkness or night that is *not at all sinister*, and that we easily overlook when our notions of light and dark lack spiritual subtlety. St. John of the Cross, for instance, wrote of a twofold "dark night of the soul" which includes a night of the senses, as well as a night of the ratiocinating mind or intellect. The mystic lover-of-wisdom cultivates both of these nights, initially through fastidious efforts at actively calming the senses in the first night, and then passively by awaiting a peaceful emptying-out of the mind in the second night. For the lover seeking out these sorts of night, all the myriad things, as well as all thoughts, feelings, images, and sensations that occupy the mind in its ordinary states and in the light of reason actually serve only to obscure vision of the deepest reality. And yet this dark ground of reality is precisely that source of all the deepest spiritual yearning for wisdom in the soul.

Putting aside St. John of the Cross, in this reflection on teaching, I want to consider Friedrich Nietzsche's famous "Night Song" from *Thus Spake Zarathustra*. The philosopher Eric Voegelin remarks that here we have the "confession" of a "spiritually sensitive man" who suffers "in the consciousness of his demonic occlusion." In Voegelin's judgment:

> [M]ystic night is denied him. He is imprisoned in the icy light of his existence. And from this prison rises the protestation – half lament, half prayer, and still not free of the defiance of the rebel – 'And my soul, too, is the song of a lover.'[3]

I find Voegelin's broader condemnation of Nietzsche as a gnostic pneumopath unconvincing, but he seems correct about how Nietzsche laments his "demonic occlusion" from "mystic night" in this tender poem. Ever since my first encounters with Nietzsche in university, I have felt a great affinity for him, perhaps because of his ability to articulate this subtle sense of spiritual privation that I too feel: the tension or "dissatisfactoriness" that creates within me an awareness *of*, or perhaps an attunement *towards* something ineffable and beautiful, something I intimate and vaguely recollect, lying just beyond the grasp of my faculties. But Nietzsche's writing is even more masterful than this; for he is able to articulate not simply our *primary* suffering awareness of this precious, subtle tension towards the ground of being; simultaneously, he gives voice to a kind of *secondary* suffering or turmoil that we undergo in experiencing the boundary between ourselves and that dark ground as an infinite one—unbridgeable by any effort of body, mind, or soul, and always finding ourselves daimonically *limited*, seemingly doomed to failure and exiled by this bare fact. This twofold state of suffering was Nietzsche's ordinary psychological state: he was a man who yearned after deep Wisdom, but one who also found himself continually falling short and incapacitated. His words in the "Night Song" give poignant voice to the pain of always being far apart from his existential Beloved, unreceptive, alone, and lacking any means of closing the distance.

I empathize with Nietzsche. I am sure that many "sensitive" readers among you feel this delightful *primary* tension towards the dark ground of which Nietzsche wrote; but perhaps you likewise suffer in the *secondary* fashion from similar feelings of daimonic limitation? And if you happen to be teachers or teachers-in-training, how does Nietzsche's "Night Song" speak to your own experiences in an educational institution? Indeed, as teachers, what does *daily immersion* in a school environment *do* to our tender souls, which are in a state much like Nietzsche's if we have cultivated some spiritual subtlety? For our souls are indeed the "songs of lovers." Let's investigate for a bit.

* * *

Nietzsche knows well that the life of the mind involves much *action* and *willing*. Thinking, after all, is a kind of *doing* or *activity*. There is, for instance, the *grasping* of things from multiple perspectives, as well as *comprehending* and *applying*. So too is there *analyzing, synthesizing, reasoning, testing, playing, warring,* and *turning things over*. There is likewise *searching, wandering, destroying, building, assessing,* and *re-evaluating*. All these *activities of the mind* in its attempts at seeing and understanding are also *activities of the will* asserting itself, driven as they are by the desire to know what Josef Pieper calls "the totality"[4] of what *is*.

But the active life of the mind in solitude is not Nietzsche's sole concern; he seeks to think these things not simply for himself *alone*. Rather, he craves fellowship and communion with others in the theoretic act of coming-to-see, to know, and to delight in affirming all that *is*. This is why Nietzsche *writes*. It is also why so much of his writing concerns friendship. Indeed, I'd hazard to say that Nietzsche viewed his writing as a kind of *ecumenical* activity inasmuch as it was for the *oikoumene*, for "the whole inhabited world," or at least for those few spread out across the whole inhabited world who can find some resonance in their own souls with what he has written.

Nietzsche's works are a gift for those of us with sensitivities and openness towards such matters; his words are designed to draw out that vague awareness of the psychic tensions and longings that lie latent in our depths—and not simply to have us consider these tensions, but rather actively *to increase them*, even exacerbating our spiritual discomfort! In doing so, Nietzsche means to challenge all of our pretences to knowledge, and he wants to encourage us to take up Wisdom's pursuit along with him in a vicarious sort of friendship. He stands before us as the teacher *extraordinaire* who, like Socrates, has "never taught anyone anything,"[5] and who espouses no doctrine. Also like Socrates, Nietzsche calls our attention to that primary form of *suffering* or *experience* for which the Greeks had one word: *pathos*. Throughout his writings,

Nietzsche brilliantly portrays these primary experiences of spiritual *pathos* and yearning. Like Plato, Nietzsche was a master at expressing this delightful form of suffering in dramatic fashion as a kind of "suffering of the Beautiful."

However, Nietzsche is also *unlike* Socrates and more specifically *like us* as moderns in our painful awareness of the *secondary* variety of suffering mentioned above; for whereas Socrates and the ancients seem to move innocently, freely, and unimpeded in the realm of spiritual things as *daimonioi andres* or "daimonic men," we moderns find ourselves deeply fraught and weighed down by two millennia of confusions and forgetting that have rendered us daimonically un-predisposed (if not disabled!) for Wisdom's pursuit. Nietzsche speaks to us powerfully from this modern perspective. We can empathize with his suffering as beings in whom Wordsworth's "intimations of immortality" have grown so weak, or who, in feeling them, have come to find ourselves daimonically-barren in our responsiveness and in the folly of our attempts to re-connect with this great heritage of Heart that we have lost. Indeed, following Nietzsche's sentiments, what is the history of Western civilization if not a kind of diversion from Wisdom's pursuit, a descent into uncultured, inhumane barbarism, technological fanaticism, and ideological madness?

\* \* \*

So what precisely *is* Nietzsche's daimonic experience as a modern? What delicate tensions has he felt and suffered as a teacher? In his "Night Song," Nietzsche tells us:

> I live in my own light; I drink back into myself the flames that break out of me. I do not know the happiness of those who receive; and I have often dreamed that even stealing must be more blessed than receiving. This is my poverty, that my hand never rests from giving; this is my envy, that I see waiting eyes and givers! Oh, darkening of my sun! Oh, craving to crave! Oh, ravenous hunger in satiation!

Poetically, Nietzsche "confesses" to us the pain that arises from the constant activity of his will. He grieves especially his fiery nature as one who, out of necessity, orders the world and others around him. He is one who, by his willing, establishes and arranges things, leading others in developing their understanding and in formulating "revaluations." As writer, Nietzsche *gives*, and he speaks to us in the "Night Song" of his *giving-ness* as teacher; he tells us about how this *giving-ness* affects his ability to *receive* and to be *receptive*. As a tender soul, Nietzsche feels the wear-and-tear of his giving-ness, of masterful willing, and assertiveness. He feels the dominion of his will as a great impediment to his own spiritual development. Nietzsche laments the inescapable requirement he feels as teacher to give. In particular, he laments its effects upon his ability to receive, to be passive or open, and to be affected by the transcendent things given to night.

\* \* \*

> They receive from me, but do I touch their souls? There is a cleft between giving and receiving; and the narrowest cleft is the last to be bridged. A hunger grows out of my beauty: I should like to hurt those for whom I shine; I should like to rob those to whom I give; thus do I hunger for malice. To withdraw my hand when the other hand already reaches out to it; to linger like the waterfall, which lingers even while it plunges: thus do I hunger for malice. Such revenge my fullness plots: such spite wells up out of my loneliness. My happiness in giving died in giving; my virtue tired of itself in its overflow.

Always seeking ways to unsettle us, Nietzsche intentionally turns the words of Jesus-the-teacher inside out: "It is more blessed to give than to receive" (*Acts* 20:35). In his "Night Song," Nietzsche shows us how the exercise of our will in spilling forth like a waterfall and in *giving* may not, in fact, provide access to the deepest reality of the soul, which cannot be touched through any *activity* of the will, but is grasped only in utter stillness.

*Loving and serving one's neighbour*—for instance, a student—is said by Christ to be identical with *loving God* (Matthew 22:36–40), these being the two greatest commandments. In a similar vein, elsewhere Jesus preaches, "Truly I tell you, just as you did it to one of the least of these who are members of my family, you did it to me" (Matthew 25:40). Clearly, loving one's neighbour and the love of God are equated in these passages. However, in Nietzsche's "Night Song," the will's active service towards others is experienced as an *impediment* to cultivating the passivity with which one *receives* in the dark night; one whose will is busy administering, organizing, assisting, and attending to other ends (say, the needs of our students) is clearly not dwelling in the passive receptivity of one who has been emptied out of all wilfulness; indeed, the will's *activity* runs counter to the cultivation of *stillness*, and with it, the readiness to receive or to be filled up with grace as a freely given gift. This is the "cleft" of which Nietzsche speaks between *giving* and *receiving*; his poetry in the "Night Song" articulates an insight not dissimilar to the observations offered by the anonymous author of the medieval *Cloud of Unknowing* who writes that the wilfulness of the "I" or the ego is the last and greatest impediment between you and your God:

> [W]hat remains between you and your God is a simple knowing and feeling of your own being. This knowing and feeling must always be destroyed, before it is possible for you to experience in truth the perfection of this exercise.[6]

In other words, one who must, by the demands of his or her chosen profession, always remain assertive and "in charge," and who is called upon to look to the exercise of the will as the source for all meaning will necessarily find himself or herself bereft of all possibility for intimate contemplative union. Nietzsche feels his daimonic limitation in relation to this contemplative "exercise" in passivity. There is, in his poetry, a confession of Nietzsche's own feelings of unworthiness for such gifts as one who is all light, and therefore unable to find embrace in the dark night of the soul.

But what of Nietzsche's "malice"—of his desire to "hurt" and to rob? These are but rhetorical flourishes the poet uses to provoke our moral outrage, to awaken us from our unquestioning slumber, and then hopefully, to make us wonder, "Whatever could he mean?" Simply put: Nietzsche wants nothing more than to refrain from the personal willing and self-assertion of one who experiences his own will as the source of all meaning, and rather to allow the contemplative, theoretic gaze upon what *is* to inform his being.

Essentially, Nietzsche seeks to leave behind the basic "constructivist" tenet preached at virtually every Teacher's College nowadays—namely, that all meaning and truth is "made" or constructed, and that all order is derived from the exertion of one's own will upon oneself, upon others, and upon the world around oneself. Abstractly, this "constructivist" viewpoint *seems* liberating, for it claims to release us from the bondage of grand social dogmas and oppressive ideologies masquerading as truth; it deigns, moreover, to establish each of us as our *own* originators for meaning, and hence to provide every one of us with infinite possibilities. Nietzsche, however, has plumbed the depths of these promises experientially, and he recognizes their "light" as a cold, hollow one to live by. In his "Night Song," Nietzsche clearly yearns for more than this cold light; but he finds that his daily, wilful manner of being and acting in the world, his experience of himself, and his personal limitations all prevent him from being able to transcend the closedness inherent in the constructivist perspective.

* * *

> The danger of those who always give is that they lose their sense of shame; and the heart and hand of those who always mete out become callous from always meting out. My eye no longer wells over at the shame of those who beg; my hand has grown too hard for the trembling of filled hands. Where have the tears of my eyes gone and the down of my heart? Oh, the loneliness of all givers! Oh, the taciturnity of all who shine!

What are the consequences of living and teaching from within a constructivist paradigm, where *meaning-making*, or giving, willing, and ordering are everything? Nietzsche tells us in short order: we "lose our sense of shame." As a classical philologist, Nietzsche is all too familiar with the Greek word for shame: *aidos*. At its most easily identified level, *aidos* connotes a kind of fear about what others will think of us when we misstep. In this regard, *aidos* is simply a control mechanism for the maintenance of social order. Nietzsche is not concerned with this sort of shame. However, on a more profound level, *aidos* can also mean "awe"—that wonder of the opened soul in the face of the overwhelming and the divine. This is the forsaken *aidos* that Nietzsche laments in the "Night Song." His poem speaks of a refined sensitivity and an opening awareness that is lost through the will's constant toil and by the attrition wrought in all-consuming activity. The wear-and-tear of needing always to act, to give, to manage, and to direct is "callous-forming"; the eye, a timeless symbol for our contemplative capacities, no longer feels any receptivity or attunement, nor does the hand know the joy of receiving freely the divine gifts which are available to anyone able to enter into the dark night.

These men and women of light, these stars who shine with their icy light for others to receive; these teachers know nothing of the very community they would seek to formulate through their giving: "cold against suns – thus moves every sun." Hence, Nietzsche's "loneliness."

The poet-philosopher finds in his "Night Song" something deeply counter-productive, self-defeating, and impotent in the muscular *will to power* argumentation so often attributed to him, but most especially in the broadly accepted assumption that the teaching life should be "student-centered" service, or that proper teaching is best characterized as being "*all* for the children."

Teaching is a highly active, service-towards-others endeavour; but without a complementary (and foundational!) involvement in the contemplative life (*vita contemplativa*), all the neighbourly efforts exerted in the active life (*vita activa*) of the teacher are akin to the cold light of a lonely star. Teachers become alienated and lonely centres of willing; seeking out and fostering community, they find themselves bereft of any seeing (*theoria*) that would enable them to intimate their true community with being, which comes to us as gift, and only through the receptivity we have cultivated in our souls. Without any existential feeling of belonging to this communion of being, lacking any intimate connection in joy to this unity, how genuine are these platitudinous "communities of learning" that we endeavour to construct (and that we are mandated to build!) in our classrooms?

Always serving, always identifying learner needs and objectives, always diagnosing problems, developing strategies and programs-of-work to address learning, always seeing by means of a kind of "shorthand" in order to administer to so many students all at once, always doing and acting and willing: it is easy to see how, as teachers, we become like Nietzsche's isolated stars, hardened through vigorous giving to the receipt of spiritual gifts: "The suns fly like a storm in their orbits: that is their motion. They follow their inexorable will: that is their coldness." However, real warmth, Nietzsche contends poetically, comes not from the icy, isolated, fiery will racing forth along its orbit, but from the silence and stillness of pervading night—a darkness that penetrates all but the stars, who find themselves bereft of this true warmth as a consequence: "Oh, it is only you, you dark ones, you nocturnal ones, who create warmth out of that which shines." Nietzsche would have us find ways of allowing the warmth of that dark night to inhabit us. And yet, once we have acknowledged the "cleft" between giving and receiving, how can the requisite receptivity be nurtured in the active life of a teacher?

\* \* \*

From within a teacher's lived experiences, think for yourselves about the ways that Nietzsche's "Night Song" relates to your own personal situation. Does his poem speak to your spiritual yearnings—perhaps how your life as a teacher occasionally leads you to suffer either in the delightful awareness of these subtle tensions, or perhaps from the *fear* of losing any sense for them? Nietzsche is not unlike the best ancient and medieval writers who have thoughtfully observed that *genuine teaching* is not simply a profession or a job; more profoundly, it is a "way of life"—*two* ways of life, in fact. That is to say: contrary to what we are told in Teacher's College, by school boards, licensing bodies, and educational "experts," teaching is *not* simply the "active life" of service towards students and the community; foundationally, it *must* remain genuinely and consciously grounded in the "contemplative life." It must be animated by a fundamental spiritual desire that seeks deep union with what *is* through the cultivation of understanding. This *eros* is what Nietzsche referred to elsewhere as *amor Fati*[7]; it is what he calls in *Zarathustra* our shared human heritage—namely, our elusive capacity for joy that "wants deep Eternity."[8]

Nietzsche's "Night Song" resonates deeply with me as an educator. At its best, teaching is a beautiful, light-filled job that calls us into community with others; the school is a place where we can pursue the truth about what *is* contemplatively while simultaneously cultivating selflessness and humility in the flurry of our active service towards others. Teaching is a transformative life path, and we are so lucky to be teachers!

And yet, there is certainly a tendency towards spiritual decay in teaching. Addressing the problem of this modern spiritual malaise, Nietzsche helps us to recognize as its cause the manner in which our willing, administering, and ordering activities are apt to become all-consuming. As teachers, we easily become lost in our days—in the giving and in the speed with which we must move from one thing to the next, from one problem or challenge to the next, from one child to the next. We learn a kind of short-hand in our dealings with each other, with students, with problems, and with our subject matters. We cease really to see who or what stands in front of us; we cease to yearn for the truth about the matters we are studying, having already grown to be "experts" in them; we become accustomed to the most efficient and effective manners of assessment; we learn quickly how to diagnose educational difficulties, as well as to lead students towards the mandated "outcomes" in their learning trajectories. Through the years, our eyes can become very good and efficient *seers* in the shallow, needful ways mandated for professional competence, but dull and blind to the deeper things about others and ourselves. We continue to give as we have always given, but the "callouses" of which Nietzsche speaks gradually cover over our souls. We become numbed to the *vita contemplativa* by the demands of teaching; we grow unfeeling towards that intimate love of truth and desire to know what *is*, which must always underpin a healthy *vita activa*. Hence, one day we find ourselves standing amidst a classroom "community of learners" that we have forged through the bent of our masterful will; but we stand there only as a *stranger* to true community, not knowing our own true self or the true selves of our students, unable to connect or to feel connected on a deeper level, lacking the receptivity or passivity needed to enter into the dark night in which such things are known.

There is, in short, a deep and urgent spiritual need for a properly contemplative, wisdom-seeking environment in schools. Teachers, school boards and administrators, students and parents, university faculties of education and education policy makers regularly fail to understand this. They *appear* to see the "active life" of the teacher clearly enough, but they make its claims upon the "teaching profession" hegemonic and all-consuming, which has the self-defeating effect of emptying the teacher's *vita activa* of its spiritual grounding in the contemplative urge to know and to love what *is*. *This needs to change.* Put another way: our current manner of structuring teaching and education exacerbates and inflames the secondary, modern form of suffering discussed above while simultaneously deadening our awareness of that ancient, timeless, and *primary* suffering of the Beautiful that is our heritage and birthright as human beings. Until education policy makers, education systems, and the teachers who populate these systems grow in their understanding of the poetic truths spoken by Nietzsche in his "Night Song," our plight as teachers who suffer in our own icy light for want of the warmth received only in darkness can do nothing but continue.

## Notes

1. For instance, see Sean Steel, "Schooling for 'Deep Knowing': On the Education of a Pithecanthropus Erectus," *Humanitas* 29, no. 1/2 (2016): 133–55; Steel, "The Birth of Dionysian Education (Out of the Spirit of Music)? Part Two," *Philosophy of Music Education Review* 23, no. 1 (2015): 67–81; Steel, "On the High School Education of a Pithecanthropus Erectus," *The High School Journal* 98, no. 1 (2014): 5–21; Steel, "The Birth of Dionysian Education (Out of the Spirit of Music)? Part One," *Philosophy of Music Education Review* 22, no. 1 (2014): 38–60. https://doi.org/10.2979/philmusieducrevi.22.1.38; and Steel, "On the Need for Dionysian Education in Schools Today," *Educational Theory* 64, no. 2 (2014): 123–41. For a thoughtful analysis of this approach to thinking about Nietzsche's philosophy in relation to education see the podcast by Thaddeus Kozinski, entitled, "Dionysus, Apollo, and the Challenge of Deep Knowing," in *The After Dinner Scholar* (Wyoming Catholic College, October 10, 2017), https://wyomingcatholiccollege.podbean.com/e/dionysus-apollo-and-the-challenge-of-deep-knowing-with-dr-thaddeus-kozinski/.
2. All quotes from the "Night Song" in *Thus Spake Zarathustra* are taken from Friedrich Nietzsche, *The Portable Nietzsche*, ed. and trans. Walter Kaufmann (London: Penguin, 1976), II.9.
3. Eric Voegelin, *Science, Politics and Gnosticism* (Washington, DC: Regnery Publishing, 1997), 21.
4. Josef Pieper, *In Defence of Philosophy: Classical Wisdom Stands Up to Modern Challenges*, trans. Lothar Krauth (San Francisco: Ignatius Press, 1966), 12.
5. A paraphrase of Socrates' words in Plato's *Apology* 33a.
6. Anonymous, *The Cloud of Unknowing*, ed. James Walsh (Ramsey, NJ: Paulist Press, 1981), XLII.
7. See Section 10 of Friedrich Nietzsche, "Why I Am So Clever," in *Ecce Homo*, trans. Walter Kaufmann (New York: Vintage Books, 1967). Also aphorism 1041 in Friedrich Nietzsche, *The Will to Power*, trans. Walter Kaufmann and R. J. Hollingdale (New York: Vintage Books, 1967).
8. Nietzsche, "The Other Dancing Song," in *Zarathustra*, Section 3.

## References

Anonymous. *The Cloud of Unknowing*. Ed. James Walsh. Ramsey, NJ: Paulist Press, 1981.

Kozinski, Thaddeus. "Dionysus, Apollo, and the Challenge of Deep Knowing." Podcast in *The After Dinner Scholar*. Wyoming Catholic College, October 10, 2017. https://wyomingcatholiccollege.podbean.com/e/dionysus-apollo-and-the-challenge-of-deep-knowing-with-dr-thaddeus-kozinski/.

Nietzsche, Friedrich. *Ecce Homo*. Trans. Walter Kaufmann. New York: Vintage Books, 1967.
Nietzsche, Friedrich. *The Will to Power*. Trans. Walter Kaufmann and R. J. Hollingdale. New York: Vintage Books, 1967.
Nietzsche, Friedrich. *The Portable Nietzsche*. Ed. and trans. Walter Kaufmann. London: Penguin, 1976.
Pieper, Josef. *In Defence of Philosophy: Classical Wisdom Stands Up to Modern Challenges*. Trans. Lothar Krauth. San Francisco: Ignatius Press, 1966.
Steel, Sean. "On the High School Education of a Pithecanthropus Erectus." *The High School Journal* 98 no. 1 (2014): 5–21.
Steel, Sean. "On the Need for Dionysian Education in Schools Today." *Educational Theory* 64 no. 2 (2014): 123–41.
Steel, Sean. "The Birth of Dionysian Education (Out of the Spirit of Music)? Part One." *Philosophy of Music Education Review* 22 no. 1 (2014): 38–60. https://doi.org/10.2979/philmusieducrevi.22.1.38.
Steel, Sean. "The Birth of Dionysian Education (Out of the Spirit of Music)? Part Two." *Philosophy of Music Education Review* 23, no. 1 (2015): 67–81.
Steel, Sean. "Schooling for 'Deep Knowing': On the Education of a Pithecanthropus Erectus." *Humanitas* 29, no. 1/2 (2016): 133–55.
Voegelin, Eric. *Science, Politics and Gnosticism*. Washington, DC: Regnery Publishing, 1997.

# a shoreline to stand on

### *Daniela Elza*

the mist       pauses      (only for an instant
in the elbow of the mountain

the thin blue horizon—     a vein that opens up
into our dreams

you look into the distance      to where
a new order      might emerge      might

make itself     apparent.

what is the sound     of one mind     filled
with wonder?

of a hand reaching for     the golden lines
racing     along the shallow bottom of a lake?

the map we got at the corner store is
                       useless here.

---

D. Elza (✉)
Vancouver, BC, Canada
e-mail: daniela@livingcode.org

> it does not mark the place where    you ran
> your fingers    through the ivy    and the rustling
>
> did not just remind you    but turned you    into
>
> ## rain.
>
> poetry is    this at*tempt*    to k*now*
>
> how    *these words*    become
>           *a shoreline*    *we can stand on*

These words / a shoreline where we can stand.
—James Gurley.[1]

---

First published in *the weight of dew* (Mother Tongue Publishing, 2012). Poem reprinted with permission from author.

[1] Gurley, J. (2002). *Human Cartography*. Kirksville, Missouri: Truman State University Press.

# Chapter 12:
# "Living in the Shadow of What I Teach," or Rather, "Learning from Our Needs"

*Stefan Gillow Reynolds*

I once asked a colleague of mine at Georgetown University when we were teaching a course on "Mysticism in the World Religions" whether he ever felt he had to be a mystic in order to teach mysticism. He replied, "No." For him it was an academic study; he was interested in it but never felt, as a scholar of Hindu meditative practices, that he had to become a Sadhu. Besides, his wife would have had little time for that, he added. Why then do I have this nagging feeling that for my teaching to carry conviction I must walk the talk? For me, a good teacher is one whose words and whose life match up. In my subject of spirituality and mysticism I feel I have grasped the ideas, but the life is way beyond me. I am explaining to my students how to read a map, but are we really in the country represented by it? The map seems quite irrelevant if we have no intention to go there. Even in the academic study and teaching of spirituality, few of us feel we are living in "the silent land" the mystics spoke

S. G. Reynolds (✉)
Lismore, Co. Waterford, Ireland

© The Author(s) 2019
S. Steel and A. Homeniuk (eds.),
*Suffering and the Intelligence of Love in the Teaching Life*,
https://doi.org/10.1007/978-3-030-05958-3_19

about. Really, my job should be to encourage students to try to go to that country and then the maps will make more sense. We would know what we live, and live out what we know.

St. John of the Cross once said that all his writings on the spiritual life were just the shadow cast by the light of God. Can we know the light from the shadow? Certainly, we know which way the light shines from which way the shadow falls. In fact, we know how close we are to the light source by the extent of the shadow. The closer we are, the greater the shadow—the more there is to learn. And there would be no shadow if we were not there. Am I as a teacher standing in the way? Am I living in the shadow of what I teach? But then, as a tour guide to an unknown land, I would orientate myself only by which way the shadow lies and, like a sundial, tell the time from what points away from the sun. In the end, I am learning that this is not a bad thing; in fact, I believe we only really learn through our sense of distance. Only when we realise our need, our ignorance, our unexamined prejudices, do we turn and yearn for a fuller knowing. I'll try to explain.

If spirituality is a science of the soul then, just as science tries to be empirical through actual experiments, so we must come to "spirit" from experience, not just book learning. There are problems with this view, however, that lie at the root of my learned colleague distancing himself from the notion that he had to be a mystic to teach mysticism: (1) Academic learning is supposed to be objective without too much interference from subjective experience or confessional viewpoints; (2) Most of the mystics, in fact, put rather small emphasis on book learning, so if we really practiced what they preached we wouldn't be scholars anyway; and (3) if we really wanted to live the life of the people we were teaching about we would go off to the desert, be unclothed or at least discalced, retire to a monastery or some other venue and spend large amounts of time emptying our minds of unnecessary knowledge. In other words, if we were mystics we wouldn't be doing what we are doing as teachers: educating our students so that they can earn high grades and acquire good jobs.

My learned colleague is correct about these things, and my suffering as a teacher is that I can't be happy with that state of affairs. I am troubled by this gap between what I teach and what I am. I feel like a pundit merely debating ideas, when real insight comes from the transmission of a lived experience, or rather getting students to reflect on their own experience. The mystics all seem to say the truth is within us, so at times

I have the feeling that everything I teach only gets in the way. It is a subject which particularly demands a maieutic method rather than just remembering information. I have asked friends who teach other less esoteric subjects—math, science, or English—whether they feel the same doubts and inadequacy: "If we know that we aren't wise, can we stand before others as 'teachers'?" They tend to look at me rather askance, as if I were trying to impose a moral rectitude as a qualification for teaching! A teacher need not be a guru. He or she merely has to raise student interest. However, some of my colleagues have felt that their own lack of interest in the subjects they teach—and at honest moments we can all admit we are bored by a repetitive syllabus—make it hard really to inspire others. It seems to be agreed that interest in any subject is rather caught than taught. Imperfections and flaws of character in teachers are much less of a detriment than lack of enthusiasm for what they teach. Enthusiasm comes from a certain yearning to understand something. Is it possible to keep this yearning in the face of the practical pressures of the teaching profession?

In my more balanced moments I know that religious traditions and the witness of those who have walked the path of prayer are a motivation for our own practice. But in teaching about the mystics of the world religions I am not encouraged to hold them up seriously as models of imitation. I don't really want my students to leave their studies becoming "learnedly ignorant and wisely unlearned," as Gregory the Great says of St. Benedict when he left his collegial studies in Rome to live in a cave in the fifth century. Nor, when teaching theology, do I want them to take too seriously the conviction of the medieval text, *The Cloud of Unknowing*, that thought is simply useless in knowing God. In my talks on the wonders of St. Francis of Assisi, if I ever persuaded a student actually to imitate him in renouncing the values of the world I would, no doubt, be in trouble with his or her parents. My role as a teacher is to interest and engage students, but the ultimate measuring stick for a successful course is good exam results, not levels of sanctity.

We often hear that education in good institutions must be for the "whole person," and not just for the mind. Normally this means that there is a supposedly healthy dose of sport. However, if we were to take this concern for wholeness seriously, then we would need to look at not only the body and the mind, but also the spirit. But how can we be really teaching if this sidelined spiritual aspect and the search for wholeness is what is at the heart of education? Moreover, can one really emphasise wholeness when that may lessen the impetus to drive our students to be productive, successful, and ambitious in their working lives? Can we really take St. Paul's dictum seriously in our teaching, that "we should have no ambition except to do good" (Titus 2:11–14)? To treat learning as somehow contradictory to faith, or to a good life, is also to deny the wholeness of the human person. There is something in us, I am convinced, that *longs* to learn, if only that longing can be uncovered. I feel it is a longing not just for ourselves but for others. It is a longing, therefore, that has much to do with the impulse to teach.

Coming back to my subject, from an educator's point of view, the problem with the mystics and saints of the world religions is that they are often so radical, and I know students can be looking for that radicalism. I even empathise with such students because back when I was a student, it entered my head that I wanted to be a monk. The idea soon left my head after falling in love during my last year. Monasteries, though not particularly approved as career choices, offer the possibility for a sort of respectable contemplative radicalism; but there are other forms of radicalism associated with religion, which as teachers we really don't want to inculcate, such as the narrow-mindedness that thinks it can know without learning, or that it has a right to impose "truth" on others without being a disciple of truth oneself. So the best way is to approach "religious enthusiasm," even in its most contemplative form, with the detached curiosity and temperance of a scholar.

I therefore find myself asking students to compare and contrast different religious phenomena so they learn to evaluate things in terms of other things: Buddhism in terms of Christianity; Islam as a religion of Abraham; otherness and sameness, but never totally other. We don't want anyone in the group to become totally other; that is outside the dialogue that is the key to learning. Western education wants all of us, whatever our commitments, to be children of the Enlightenment, and quite rightly, insofar as scepticism towards universal truth claims is a good antidote to sectarian viewpoints. But to claim that the default starting point for learning has to be a detached rationalism is also an attempt to subsume cultural differences and other diverse approaches to learning. In the Middle Ages, for example, doubt and scepticism were not felt to be good seed-grounds for intellectual inquiry. "Faith seeking understanding" was the maxim for learning. We live in different times, but ways of learning will be different for different people.

The importance of respecting each student's way of engaging is, I have felt, key to my reticence in ever expecting my students to want to be mystics. My own interest in the "experience" of mysticism rather than just the study I have to accept is also personal; it shouldn't be expected from my teaching colleagues in Religious Studies. However, the idea that teaching is a "way of life" rather than just a profession that lasts from 9 to 5 is, I think, a pre-requisite for good teaching that inspires others.

\* \* \*

How do teachers of mysticism and spirituality live up to what they teach? My studies make me aware of the gap between my life and that of the mystics. At times, the saints I study seem less like models for imitation than something to which I can never match up. They infiltrate what Freud called the super-ego—that part of our psyche which loves telling us what we *should be*, but also what we are *not*. I feel its judgments when I go from teaching about the Desert Fathers and Mothers who went out to live in the Egyptian desert in the fourth century to a faculty party where there is far from a drought of drink. Or again: when I talk about the celibacy of monks and nuns (which for a lot of Christian history was seen as a prerequisite for contemplation), but then my wife has cooked me a surprise dinner at home and the music is on. Now, I shouldn't exaggerate; Christianity has changed, but I am drawn towards thinking and teaching a lot of these older elements.

I read about people rising up very early to spend long hours in prayer and fasting, giving away all they have, kissing lepers, being hung, drawn, and quartered for their faith, or falling into ecstasy. Well, it would have to be a very "good day" for me to do any of those things (and that value judgement in itself shows the spiritual super-ego peeping over my quotidian shoulder). As a married lay person with only moderate self-discipline, and as a teacher about monastic and mystical spirituality I have often felt the tension and contradiction between myself and what I teach. I know God uses us in our weakness, and that a broken jar lets in the light. But the question whether I can teach spirituality and wisdom without feeling particularly spiritual or wise remains.

Admittedly, my teaching is about what some of my friends call "the highfalutin stuff"—that is, the very best and greatest thinkers and spiritual writers. My colleagues seem not to experience the same super-ego presence when talking about the "nuts and bolts" or technical-type courses that make up a lot of teaching curriculum. However, I still feel that it is not my subject that creates this different problem for me. The moment any of us start going deep with education, our positions as teachers become problematic. And it is this problematic part—because it is all about our longing for authenticity, for more understanding, for wholeness—that is the very best and most important part of teaching, learning, and education.

We often hear it said about teachers that, "We teach from who we are," or even "We teach who we are." That sounds correct to me. But then, in my subject, it often appears to me that I am teaching as an outsider about what I am *not*. And yet, if the longing for spiritual wisdom is part of who I am, then am I teaching about who I am when I teach about the great saints? I am called to be a teacher and not a desert monk, or missionary of charity; and yet in my longing to be whole I am deeply connected to that spiritual life which seems to elude me.

I often teach about a particular mystic, Thèrese of Lisieux, who was called to be an enclosed nun, and yet she longed to be a missionary, a martyr, a doctor, and a priest. She had read about the lives of the great saints, and she suffered from a sense of her own unfruitfulness and mediocre life in comparison with them. However, she realised in the end that her longing was itself a participation in those callings, and she felt able to help others in fulfilling their ministries from within her cloister. She corresponded with missionaries and priests, giving them encouragement and praying for them. As teachers, we have a little of that role: encouraging and facilitating our students to find their way.

In this sense, our suffering from "enclosure," or the feeling of being confined within a set curriculum coupled with the awareness of our "distance" from the field of action in the world, is illusory. The teacher of maths is linked to the theoretical physicist through a community of interest; teachers of medicine are linked through their shared concern with doctors and nurses; the English teacher revels in the same creativity of language as the play-write and the poet; and Religious Education teachers are by the nature of their work in communion with the saints. I suspect it's the ego which makes us feel separate and inferior. The Kingdom of God is within us all. Thou art that. All of us are *tathagatagarbha*, or Buddha nature.

There is a kind of suffering that arises from our longing for the Beautiful, for the Sublime, and for the Good. Plato believed that love is a kind of suffering in the awareness of Goodness. Such longing may feel like it is in tension with the mundanity of teaching a subject that we may be long familiar with and maybe even a little tired of; but it is this longing which is a sign that the subject is still alive to us. We still seek for the beauty of the complete mathematic equation, for the wonder of the natural world revealed in science, and for the goodness of human nature witnessed in the lives of saints.

* * *

In recent years I have more and more changed the context of where I teach. This is not so much due to choice as to demand. Theology is no longer a vastly popular subject at University, even less so in Europe than in America. When my wife and I moved to Ireland, I found it difficult to land a teaching post at Irish universities. But I discovered a great demand in another area: retreat work. So I started leading retreat days in Parishes, at retreat houses and monasteries in Ireland. Then, through a long-term association with the World Community for Christian Meditation, I began to give retreats in other countries throughout Europe. This change may have been influenced by my suspicion that education as a means toward earning qualifications and inculcating "success paradigms"—with all the imperatives and pressures these ends entail—is deeply unsatisfactory. Retreat teaching, by contrast, is much more clearly orientated to "wholeness" and the well-being rather than the productivity of the learner. Life skills are not just cognitive. Retreat teaching involves looking at relationships, bodily health, diet, forgiveness, practices of mindfulness and meditation, prayer, as well as study. The sad thing is that retreat experiences reach relatively few young people whereas mainstream education, despite its pressures and agendas, does.

Retreat work is not nearly so onerous as working within the university academy, which has changed so much in recent years with its emphasis on accountability and endless assessment. I am grateful for my lighter teaching load, and for my rich interactions with smaller numbers of students; but I am also sorry not to be of more help to the younger generations. The difficulty of retreat work, also, is that it is itinerant; I have to move around and travel abroad a lot, which takes its toll on a stable life. It is also irregular in terms of earnings; I must be self-employed, willing to face all the complexities of tax and lack of pension. But there is a growing interest now in meditation and mindfulness, and I have been able to adapt both my teaching curriculum and doctoral studies to a more "experiential" approach towards learning that is what retreats are about. During these sessions, the aim is not to earn some qualification, but to grow in wholeness and holiness. I have always felt that God is more a way of life than a subject of discussion and argument.

I still believe it is possible to find pleasure, meaning, and fulfilment in school and university, and teaching in a more traditional classroom environment. I feel that the sense of distance from what we teach should not lead to cynicism or a withering away of enthusiasm for "holy things." When we find ourselves bogged down in class assessments, if we can keep alive that sense of longing or suffering for the Sublime, then we will also keep the lifeline open to what is really important in our teaching vocation. We will inevitably transmit that desire for more to our students: having linked the learning tasks we are given to wider horizons of meaning, we can come to wholeness not through avoiding the particular and sometimes tedious demands of each day, but through doing these things well.

A sense of the inadequacy of what we teach in relation to all there is to be learned is not a bad thing. It is the source of humility and wonder. Such a sense should not be paralyzing if we remember that learning is communal. Student and teacher, lecturer and colleagues in the academy, educator and researcher, the theorist and those who apply learning in their professions are all linked in a common endeavour. Any culture of learning is a collaboration. It could be healthy for teachers to feel that they are still students. Certainly the assimilation of different viewpoints is a fruitful form of humility. To take in the inter-personal aspect of learning will lessen the onus we might feel to be "perfect" teachers. It is clear we can only teach to the extent that others are willing to learn. Moreover, the feeling that we cannot change the world may help us study it better as it is. Study, in the end, has to do with facts rather than contingency. We may hope to make our students better and wiser people but we shouldn't expect more than any specific learning culture will allow. Humility is to accept the cards we have been given. Good teaching, as with card playing, doesn't expect a grand flush when circumstances mean we have to play at sixes and sevens. Sixes and sevens can still win, with patience. No teacher should expect a class of high fliers.

\* \* \*

I feel less in the shadow of what I teach nowadays, partly because in my own life I have been able to put into practice a little more of the contemplative wisdom I have studied, but more because prayer seems the natural way of learning about spirituality. I never, for example, understood

Ignatian spirituality despite working for years at Jesuit educational institutions until recently when I was able actually to do the Spiritual Exercises. Suddenly, what had seemed a daunting and inaccessible program of prayer that I only knew from texts became real and do-able. In other words, retreat work for me has brought spirituality down to earth—not so much as something to study abstractly, but as a valuable tool for better and happier living.

One way of nurturing this longing in a school environment is to have a time of silent attention at the beginning of each class. Call it meditation or just stillness; the aim is to make the actual experience of attention (which is implicit in all learning) tangible in a focused exercise. The World Community for Christian Meditation helps teachers implement this practice through giving students a chance to be still and to give their attention to one thing—in this case, a prayer word or mantra repeated silently and interiorly. By engaging in this daily practice, our sense of how we learn through giving attention begins to grow; we also gain a sense for the bigger picture of learning, which is not about learning "things," but developing understanding and insight into what is.

These daily moments of silence would cultivate the kind of longing I have spoken about. They would be an antidote for the dullness that can afflict the teacher of a repeated syllabus where accountability is more important than content. Such practices may likewise serve as a cure for the dullness that can afflict our students when all they learn seems to be for the sake of a qualification and seems to possess little intrinsic meaning. Such meditative practices are certainly possible in the classroom, and they have, in fact, been fostered in both public and religious schools throughout the world. These exercises in silence are a practical way of bringing spirituality down to earth and making it a real asset for learning. Apart from formal meditation, taking some time each day to have students simply observe something—not thinking about it, but just looking—can be an excellent preparation for the kind of attentiveness that is necessary for scientific experimentation and for artistic appreciation. Little practices like this can easily be introduced into the classroom, not as "filler" or breaks from the ardors of academia, but as ways of experiencing what it means at the roots to learn. Mindfulness has its own practices as well; for instance, paying attention to our bodily sensations while sitting in a chair, and noticing the sounds one can hear. All these exercises at the beginning of the class bring both student and teacher into the present moment, and they ready the group for any learning that will follow.

The teacher, mystic, and philosopher Simone Weil believed that developing the faculty of attention is "the real object and almost the sole interest of studies." In her essay, "Reflections on the Right Use of School Studies with a View to the Love of God," Weil argues that that attention is not to be "confused with a kind of muscular effort":

> If one says to one's pupils: "Now you must pay attention," one sees them contracting their brows, holding their breath, stiffening their muscles. If after two minutes they are asked what they have been paying attention to, they cannot reply. They have been concentrating on nothing.[1]

Attention, writes Weil, is "the greatest of all efforts perhaps", but it is a "negative effort" that involves watching, waiting, not seeking anything. Like mindfulness practice, it shouldn't make us tired. Relaxed alertness, like breathing in and breathing out, Weil says, is the best way to apply ourselves to any learning task or life situation:

> When we become tired, attention is scarcely possible any more, unless we have already had a good deal of practice. It is better to stop the endeavour altogether, to seek some relaxation, and then a little later to return again; we have to press on and loosen up alternately, just as we breathe in and out. Twenty minutes of concentrated un-tired attention is infinitely better than three hours of frowning application [...] Attention consists of suspending our thought, leaving it detached, empty and ready to be penetrated by the object.[2]

If objectivity is pedagogic then it involves learning about things in themselves, rather than our views of them. If post-modernism has taught us the need for multi-perspectival angle on any subject, it does not remove the need for an even-minded and inquisitive approach to things as they are in themselves, irrespective of the way we see them.

*  *  *

Cultivating student attention need not involve formal meditative practices. It usually means just showing how a subject relates to the students' lived experience. Over my years of study, many saints and wisdom teachers have come to life for me in real and sometimes amusing ways. I have realised that the saints are not so much models for imitation (though we can, of course, learn from their lives and teaching) as they are helpers, intercessors and, by God's arrangement, sources of grace. They are very much alive. When I give retreats in which we focus upon their lives, I now feel that I am talking about someone I know. Learning to know them as real people, I have discovered that they didn't come to holiness by having all the answers, by seeing the light or being more "sorted" than others. Holiness, I have discovered, is simply humanness well-lived.

It was a strange transition in my own life from reading about holy lives to accessing some of that holiness through prayer. This may be a rather Catholic position—no doubt influenced by my present residence in Ireland—but I think it has arisen from a recognition of my need for help. St. Anthony of Padua, that great thirteenth century scholar and preacher, is known today as the patron of lost things and impossible situations. Funnily enough, I have begun to know him better through losing my keys than through reading his sermons. He is alive and kicking. Or rather he is chief operator in the heavenly call centre for lost property petitions.

So in the end, I have discovered that I am not teaching things dead and past. And I am no longer under the shadow of "great people" with rather impossible lives: ascetics, celibates, and mystics. They have become a little more like my grandmother who I turn to when I am in trouble. Through all the ups and downs of my life she never tells me what to do, or even gives me advice; but she shows me that there is a bigger picture. The problems of life, even our very real sufferings, are not primarily things to be sorted, but opportunities for patience and for loving in the very un-sortedness of life. The value of this un-sortedness is something I think all teachers gradually learn. Teaching is a vocation that demands great patience and love.

Likewise, I have found that personal suffering in my life—the difficulties I have with myself and with others—is neither extraneous nor a hindrance to, my teaching. What we have to teach has to come in the end from the whole of us or it will seem half-hearted—a mere presentation of knowledge, and not a transmission of what it is to learn. To be professional doesn't mean leaving our humanity as we leave our car when we arrive for work, only returning to it when we climb back in the car at the end of the day. It may not be advisable to break down in tears in the classroom or to fall in love with other teachers, but to engage others we have to be real and, in the end, our hearts must be in our teaching.

The context of retreats has helped me to merge life with learning a little better. For instance, I no longer leave the aches of my body and heart outside the lecture room; rather, I try to integrate what I feel into my teaching. This does not mean that I make myself the subject of the lesson, or that I choose to teach only what is relevant to my mood; but it does mean I try to make what I am feeling a source of empathy. Empathy is an important skill when we have to relate to others, something so much part of the teacher's life. If we do not allow ourselves to feel, we will not be aware of what others are feeling. Our personal suffering, once accepted, becomes a source of compassion and wisdom. Our joy in life helps us enjoy the joy of others. There is always enough room even in the strictest of syllabus to adapt one's teaching just a little to where others are in the moment.

Although I have come to terms with many different kinds of suffering that arise in the life of the teacher, I still feel sadness that, in my retreat work, I no longer have the opportunity to respond to the needs of younger people. Indeed, it is one of the great boons of primary, secondary, and also university educators to be able to help young people at the very formative stages of their lives. How wonderful it is to instil in their lives a desire to investigate deeper things, whether they be scientific, artistic or philosophic. Such a desire to "look deeply" is the key to real learning, and it should be part of the "professional training" of all would-be teachers. Retreat work tends to be for adults. Their needs are not dissimilar, but I know if teachers catch the imagination of a young people with a subject, such an education gives them something they can run with throughout their entire life. Retreat work, by contrast, is more like repair work: making good what was lacking in terms of inspiration and wholeness in earlier education. What a privilege it can be to be a source of inspiration early in someone's life. I have lost that privilege. Mind you: while not acquiring a university teaching position in Ireland seemed at first a great loss, in other ways it has been a blessing. Freed from the demands of a set syllabus and entrenched teaching aims I have been empowered to adapt my teaching to what I feel people really need.

The "sense of need" is, I feel, something educators are responding to, whether they have a consciously altruistic motive, or if they just see teaching as a job. As teachers we are essentially service providers. We serve a human need to learn, similar to how hospital workers serve a human need to be well, or politicians (hopefully) serve our need to be free and to live in peace. To serve people in their learning is at the heart of teaching. But what is most needed today is to awaken ourselves and then others to that innate need—which expresses itself as a longing—to learn. Once we are in touch with that need, then the impetus to learn is there. And more than that: when learning is experienced as a need fulfilled, then the enjoyment of learning returns. Coming to teaching and to learning from a sense of need rather than with a concern for "competencies," "learning outcomes," or results will, I believe, bring more light and less tedium into education.

I still recognise that I am living in the shadow of some truth, some beauty, and some goodness that is way beyond me. Seeing the shadows of what I don't know is my best connection with the sun. Our sense of inadequacy as teachers may be our greatest guide to how we encourage others to learn. How, and toward what direction, the sun is shining is revealed by the shadows. Learning is not just about achieving success, it is about overcoming difficulties. Even (and maybe especially) in theological learning we still "see as through a glass darkly."

The shadow is not only from the "there is always more" nature of everything we teach (in whatever subject); it also stems from our necessary human limitations. We don't have all the time or patience in the world to respond to every student in the way they need. Teachers may provide tools for life's journey, training of the mind and resources for learning, but they don't provide final answers. Each student will have to apply what they learn in their own unique life and distinctive approach to studies. What we can pass on as teachers is a model of what it is to be always learning: a pedagogic stance where we are always reaching for the "more" which we know we need for any complete understanding. From the time of Socrates, it was felt that the desire to learn comes from recognising what we don't know. To instil that desire remains the great work of teachers, but involves recognising that we learn from our needs rather than our achievements.

## Notes

1. Simone Weil, "Reflections on the Right Use of School Studies with a View to the Love of God," in *Waiting on God* (London: Routledge & Kegan Paul, 1951), 54.
2. Ibid., 55–56.

## REFERENCES

The *New Oxford Annotated Bible*. New Revised Standard Version. Ed. Bruce M. Metzger and Roland E. Murphy. New York: Oxford University Press, 1991.

Weil, Simone. "Reflections on the Right Use of School Studies with a View to the Love of God." In *Waiting on God*. London: Routledge & Kegan Paul, 1951.

PART VI

# Suffering, Joy, and Gratitude in Teaching

# beauty is embarrassing

### *Daniela Elza*

I am working on becoming
                           an expert      on *not*
being      an expert.      a wounded bird
so to speak.
                        *

let the vertebrae enunciate
                      the skin accentuate
let them curate the exhibit you make of your mind.

how will you draw the map of your days
                      under domed temples
how will you      shake the fever
         the television snow  will not cool down
amidst    the planes of war     that do not      stop
dropping
         through silences      the dead keep
                                   sacred.
          how will you?
when the bitter water closes  around your ankles
like shackles.

---

D. Elza (✉)
Vancouver, BC, Canada
e-mail: daniela@livingcode.org

© The Author(s) 2019
S. Steel and A. Homeniuk (eds.),
*Suffering and the Intelligence of Love in the Teaching Life*,
https://doi.org/10.1007/978-3-030-05958-3_20

how will you step in further?

      \*

this morning    I woke up with       the crows
            (is what I was trying to tell you last night.
my heart—      a monk    facing monastery walls.
what if you stopped thinking
                  this is you?
stop thinking    you are separate from   these crows.
how will you
          speak the despair     you wake up with
the desire   that unbuttons   into your day?
        (is what I meant to ask you     tomorrow.

matters of the heart are never     simple     you say.
you say   your heart is a *dark hole*   *a wounded bird*
an *Icarus flying*   *too close to the sun.*

yet the sun   still    fanfares through this  stone city
splashes it   in its brightest colours.
                      sprouts green
through the tiny vertebrae of spring.
and a wounded bird can heal      I said.

           and look at *you*
your pockets full of folded stories      you keep
skipping   across bitter water.

         how will you    catch yourself
when life hurls you
                      over the edge?
   how will you reclaim your body
                    as an instrument
for singing the world   again?

      \*

we finger our artistic spectrums.   search for
the right metaphors   to say:
           *Eros*     *is*   *freedom.*
to say   spirit   is not   another matter
and for that

```
                        matter       is full of spirit.
    to know yourself    as you are
                                when you are loved.
    perfect             that is.
                  then learn     no one     is    perfect.

                             *

    still      all you want is      to go back     go back and
    rewrite         your unforgiving life.
    your words         will never be      good enough.

                             *

    punctuation turns        sunshine       streams down
    your shoulder            in a walled-in city.
    meaning to say
                       *nothing.*      just
    *stop.*    *pause.*         *exclaim.*              ellipses
    walking away from      a crowded history
           too intimate    to question         or name.

                             *

    today all we can do is      imagine    going through
    the Museum of Apologies.
                    (nauseated     but still interested.
    see
    how we get it       wrong       again      and again.
    learn     how to say      *sorry.*  (in this sorry drought.
              how      to remember You
                                     are my other Me.
                             *
    I am working on becoming          an expert on
       not       being      an expert—
                       a birded wound       so to speak—
    because    we need to
                         figure things out.
```

First appeared in *POIESIS: a journal of arts and communication*, Volume 15, 2013. Poem reprinted with permission from author.

# Chapter 13: Never Quite Enough

## Tom Flanagan

When Sean Steel first asked me to write something on the theme of "Suffering in Teaching," I didn't see how I could agree. My half century of university teaching, mainly at the University of Calgary but with visiting positions at a few other universities, has always been enjoyable, sometimes even exhilarating. I've been paid well to deal with fresh-faced young people in pleasant surroundings. I got to teach a discipline, in my case political science, that I entered because I found it fascinating. Where's the suffering? What's not to like? I did have one bad experience, described in my book *Persona Non Grata*; but although that took place on a university campus, it didn't arise out of teaching as such. I was giving a town-and-gown lecture when I was targeted for reprisals because of my research and participation in politics. My real students back at my home campus were nothing but supportive.

However, after a further conversation with Sean, I found that I might have something to say on this topic. There is, indeed, a chronic aspect of dissatisfaction involved in university teaching (probably at all levels of teaching, but my only experience has been in universities). I wouldn't call it suffering, rather a nagging ache, a sort of unfulfilled desire.

---

T. Flanagan (✉)
Calgary, AB, Canada
e-mail: tflanaga@ucalgary.ca

A teacher at the university level has many things in mind that he would like his students to learn. As I wrote in another context:

> Any professor worthy of his hire faces at least three challenges beyond communicating information. First, you have to awaken students' interest in topics of whose importance they have no idea and of which they probably have never even heard. Machiavelli's *Prince*. Regression equations. Supreme Court decisions. It's not so simple to make these topics compete for space in students' mind with their usual amusements of sex, drugs, and rock 'n roll.
>
> Then you want them to ask important questions about such topics. Did Machiavelli teach that the ends justify the means? Do they? Does political *raison d'état* override normal morality? What is the difference between correlation and causation? How can we use statistical controls to narrow down potential relationships between variables? How aggressive should the Supreme Court be in overturning legislation passed by Parliament? By provincial legislatures?
>
> Finally, you want to expand their horizons for future study. You want them to learn that reading old books like the *Prince* is a particularly good pathway to wisdom. Precisely because the book is so old, its context is totally different from the students' own lives, thus forcing them to grapple with essential questions without the props of familiar experience, customs, and institutions. You want them to know that regression is a basic tool in all the empirical sciences, both natural and social, and that the statistical reasoning they use in figuring out who votes for whom is fundamentally the same as the thought process involved in testing the efficacy of new medicines. And you want them to see that law is a noble intellectual enterprise, the undergirding of all civilization, not just the ticket to a lucrative career.[1]

These are ambitious goals, especially when you are simultaneously trying to teach students how to punctuate, how to footnote their papers, and in general how to express themselves clearly and succinctly. Therefore, it is not surprising that you never achieve all that you would like to. I always leave the room second-guessing myself after teaching a class, and I wake up in the middle of the night asking myself questions. Did I really get the main points across? Did I spend too much time telling the jokes and stories that help break up the intensity but can also distract from the main line of thought? Should I have put things differently?

In the same way, I'm usually not satisfied when I read term papers and final exams. Questions reverberate in my mind. Is that all I managed to communicate? Why didn't they understand my carefully selected readings?

Of course, when you think about it, there's a mismatch between professor and students. I have been working in my discipline for decades, while they are just starting out. They can't possibly absorb everything I would like to communicate, and I don't really expect them to. Nevertheless, I always have a feeling of failure, that I'm not doing the job as well as I should.

But that nagging sense of inadequacy is sometimes balanced by what happens years later. You see an article in a professional journal or a column in a newspaper written by a former student whose prose you struggled to edit, or you read about the business or political achievements of a student who may have seemed not quite with it in class, not fully understanding what you were trying to say. Or, as just happened yesterday, you get a letter from a student you haven't seen in 40 years. Then for a moment it really is all worthwhile.

## NOTE

1. Tom Flanagan, *Persona Non Grata: The Death of Free Speech in the Internet Age* (Toronto: McClelland and Stewart, 2014), 163–64.

## REFERENCE

Flanagan, Tom. *Persona Non Grata: The Death of Free Speech in the Internet Age.* Toronto: McClelland and Stewart, 2014.

# Chapter 14: Why Students Don't Suffer

*Lee Trepanier*

The best American colleges students are perhaps the most prepared, accomplished, and engaged students ever with stellar academic accomplishments and active civic engagement.[1] At the same time, they also might be the most frightened and anxious ones, too, being mediated with mood-stabilizing drugs and monitored by compliance offices about what to say and think.[2] This paradox is a reflection of the ever-widening chasm between, on the one hand, the remarkable external achievements of these students and, on the other hand, the paucity of examination about their interior lives, unless it is the therapeutic speech of empowerment and identity politics. Students seemingly move from one achievement to the next without suffering any setbacks in either external affirmations or interior reflection.

In this chapter, I will argue that the external achievements and affirmations of students and the lack of self-examination of their interior lives is a result of the university seeing them as commodities and customers rather than human beings who need cultivation. Students consequently see suffering—to be vulnerable, exposed, and unguarded—as

L. Trepanier (✉)
Saginaw Valley State University, University Center, MI, USA
e-mail: ldtrepan@svsu.edu

© The Author(s) 2019
S. Steel and A. Homeniuk (eds.),
*Suffering and the Intelligence of Love in the Teaching Life*,
https://doi.org/10.1007/978-3-030-05958-3_22

a type of personal weakness and moral failing because it does not affirm their external accomplishments. There is to be no discrepancy between the flatness of one's interior life and the mountain of achievements in the external one. To do so otherwise is tantamount to admitting failure.

The exception to this is identity politics where suffering is acceptable because of one's race, ethnicity, gender, class, or sexuality and seen as a badge of honor to be expressed in ideological cant. For those students who do not belong to a suspect class, they are expected to acknowledge and share in the suffering of these groups. But instead of generating genuine sympathy and empathy, these students only confirm their meritocratic superiority by publicly acknowledging their moral smugness in being self-aware. Rather than trying to understand the feelings and situations of the less fortunate and undertaking concrete action to help, students resort to ideological and emotive language.

In spite of their best intentions, offices of diversity need to address the problem of suffering in a way to cultivate the interior lives of all students so that they can sympathize and empathize with others. By suffering, I mean the acknowledgement of one's own inadequacy of being dependent upon another person; and by empathy, I mean the understanding and recognition of the feelings and situations of those who are less fortunate. Instead of promoting an ideological agenda, the university, with its administrators, staff, and faculty, should focus on developing the interior lives of their students under the guidance of reason, logic, and evidence. By doing so, students will recognize the gap between their external and interior lives and thereby may recognize that suffering, to sympathize and empathize, is not a sign of powerlessness but the beginning of the path towards wisdom.

## Students' Character

The best college students are excellent test-takers, have impressive resumes, and dutifully fulfill the requirements to receive an A in their classes.[3] They are respectful to authority, accept the ideology of diversity, and are advocates of social justice.[4] They are David Brooks' "organizational kids" that he had described a generation ago and are the crowning achievement of the American education system in its project to mold students' characters to be flexible, nonjudgmental, and acquisitive in accumulating various skill sets and ways of knowing.[5] They see themselves as citizens of the world and look forward to participating in a globalized economy where they can live anywhere, perform any task, and make friends with anyone.

Yet students are not motivated by a love of learning for its own sake but rather out of a fear or anxiety of being left behind in a winner-take-all world.[6] A globalized economy has made it more difficult to secure a middle-class lifestyle, the orthodoxy of diversity and groupthink has made it challenging to publicly proclaim otherwise, and the unmooring of knowledge into postmodernism has made it impossible to determine what is precious and valuable, much less what constitutes one's own self-worth.[7] Formed by a childhood of constant test-taking, scheduled activities, and technological surveillance, today's students respond by accumulating achievements upon achievements and skill set upon skill set in the effort to steel themselves against the uncertainty of their future.

In this resume arms race against one another, students are taught that suffering is a sign of weakness: to be vulnerable, exposed, and unguarded are signs of a personal and moral failing. To be left behind in the globalized economy is to be one of life's losers. Hence, the constant need and continual efforts for external affirmation—whether in social media, academic achievements, or social status—to validate their choices, career paths, and even spouses. Suffering in this sense—to acknowledge dependence upon another person and thereby recognize one's own inadequacy—is to be squeezed out at all costs in the process of college admission, summer internships, and profitable jobs afterwards.

Paradoxically, the refusal to acknowledge one's own suffering encourages a climate of empathy with the suffering of others, particularly with those who are less privileged. To understand and uphold the legitimacy of the feelings and situations of those less fortunate is to reassure students of their own sense of achievement, status, and superiority in this winner-take-all world. Emboldened by the offices of diversity on campus, students engage in identity politics and groupthink not to sympathize with the non-privileged—to recognize that the suffering and experience of others is the same as theirs—but to confirm their sense of achievement, worth, and place in the world.

Thus, the creation of "safe spaces" and embedding the ideology of diversity in university life are well-intended but misguided attempts to cultivate students' interior lives.[8] These policies are well-intended because they try to address the thoughts and feelings of students who believe themselves to be marginalized on campus, tapping into their interior life so that they, and others, can learn from it. However, these policies are misguided because they substitute ideology and emotivism instead of encouraging the use of reason and evidence to access students' interior lives, thereby treating others not as individual human beings that one can suffer, sympathize, and empathize with, but instead as groups capable of mobilization for ideological ends.

This lack of an interior life in students, where they can acknowledge their vulnerabilities and therefore the need for others, is the source of their suffering. Raised in a world of relentless external affirmations, today's students were not allowed the space to grow and develop unnoticed, with the trials, errors, and mistakes that life brings. Students live in a persistent state of fear at being noticed and shamed if caught flatfooted. Rather than risking embarrassment and humiliation, students have become nonjudgmental and nice, playing it safe where their interior life is defined and shaped almost exclusively by their external one.

Not surprisingly, the absence of a developed interior life leads students to adopt libertarianism or identity politics.[9] The ideology of libertarianism feeds into students' beliefs in meritocracy, that they deserve what they have and where they are now because of their own singular achievements, whereas identity politics gives permission to empathize with the non-privileged while, at the same time, implicitly reassure themselves of their own merit and superiority. What is missing is a genuine sense of communal politics where people can openly and civilly acknowledge, discuss, and debate their differences. What we need is a place where people can disagree without fear of *ad hominin* reprisal and see whether a common good could be achieved.

Teachers therefore must find a way to cultivate the interior life of students such that it is not dependent upon external affirmation. They should encourage students to take risks and make mistakes. One way to accomplish this is to have students realize that luck has played as much a role in forming who they are as their own efforts and abilities: their success may have been dependent upon factors beyond their control, thereby raising questions about their earned standing and superiority. And if this were the case, then being vulnerable, exposed, and unguarded may be a trait not to run away from, but instead to acknowledge and embrace. It prompts students to recognize their own inadequacies and therefore their own needs for another person.

There are a variety of ways that teachers can attempt to cultivate an interior life with an internal affirmation for students. One is to have students read certain works where authors reflect upon their own interior life: Socrates in Plato's *Apology, Crito,* and *Phaedo*; Augustine's and Rousseau's *Confessions*; Marcus Aurelius' *Meditations* and Montaigne's *Essays*; the autobiographies of Benjamin Franklin, Mahatma Gandhi, Anne Frank, and Nelson Mandela. These and similar readings can reveal to students the richness, diversity, and importance of an interior life, especially when it does not correspond to the external one. These works can provide a template for how students can reflect on their own lives.

The assignments that teachers can give to their students is another way to prompt students to think about the interiority of their lives. Whether it is journal entries, analytical essays, public presentations, or group projects, these assignments are less about mastery of the material than avenues for students to explore questions that do not have a definitive answer. Teachers consequently should evaluate these assignments with the cultivation of an interior life in mind, and allow students to revise their assignments in the hope that they learn there is nothing shameful about making a mistake or taking a risk.

If done properly, seminars, small group activities, and the Socratic Method are wonderful ways to teach students the art of inquiry and disagreement where the virtues of magnanimity, corrigibility, and civility can be learned.[10] In these modes of teachings, students can learn to sympathize and empathize with others in a way where reason, logic, and evidence are the conveyers of feelings, attitudes, and moods.[11] It is a way to show students that insight and wisdom can come by being vulnerable, exposed, and unguarded in a setting of equals.

Finally, within the confines of professional expectations and behavior, teachers should be available to meet with students individually to discuss not only their external achievements but also their interior lives. Sometimes what endures more in a student's mind is a conversation with his or her teacher rather than the content of what the student learned that semester. To be respected and loved, and to be taken seriously is what most students want as they try to figure out how to navigate their lives in the university. Whether in the classroom or during office hours, it is impossible to know which moment will have a lasting impact on a student. But if teachers can show to students that their interior life can be as rich, if not more rewarding, than their external one, they have done more than enough to help students see there is more to life than production and consumption.

## The Student as Customer

Because of the competitive demands of the globalized economy, students see themselves as customers of the university and are often treated as such by administrators, staff, and faculty.[12] The university is no longer seen as just providing academic knowledge to students, but also as begetting a social experience with rock climbing walls, computer tablets, and gourmet-style dining. Education itself is treated as a vocationalized end instead of a lifelong process of inquiry and discovery with universities transforming themselves into brands.[13] Administrators care more about student recruitment and retention than the content of student learning; thus, they spend vast amounts of time and resources trying to answer the question that parents and students have when they visit their school; namely, "What am I buying?"

With ever-increasing amounts of debt when they graduate, students are justified in asking whether their time at the university will be well worth the cost.[14] Teachers, especially those in the humanities, are not able to provide a persuasive economic reason when compared to their STEM (science, technology, engineering, and mathematics) counterparts and therefore have become obsessed with recruiting students into their programs and retaining the ones they already have.[15] Classes become infomercials that pluck students into their majors. The result is not only a further neglect of the interiority of students' lives but the reinforcement of seeing them as customers whose decision-making is driven by economic considerations.

This commodification of the classroom, where students are seen as customers, has been fostered by a culture of assessment and the promotion of technology in teaching. Students are continually assessed in quantitative metrics to confirm that they are learning, and technology is marketed as a panacea because it accommodates students' wants in flexible class schedules as well as their inclinations to use the Internet (i.e., "digital natives").[16] Teachers therefore are required to assign assessments in their classrooms—often ones that they themselves have had no share in creating—and then to write reports afterwards in order to demonstrate that their students are learning.[17] They are also incentivized by administrators with course release-time, monetary compensation, and performance evaluation to incorporate technology into the classroom.[18] Thus, the commodification of the classroom ensures that teaching is conducted in standardized, measurable units suitable for technological consumption.

In this environment, students see knowledge as a type of commodity to be packaged and sold rather than as a lived experience or enduring wisdom. The classroom is a place to be entertained, whether with a professor directly speaking to you or hidden behind a screen online. The relationship between teacher and students—and among students themselves—is seen in contractual terms. The culture of assessment and the online delivery of knowledge reinforces this customer-service perspective of education because knowledge is presented in discrete, measurable units. The messiness of knowledge, the serendipity of discovery, and the ineffableness of learning become lost in this environment of commodification, quantification, and technological assessment.

The underlying causes for this account of education are many: the increasing power of university accreditation agencies, the transformation of administrators from colleagues to managers, the neoliberal university competing for students and dollars in an era of shrinking state support, the public demand for educational accountability in a period of debt and spiraling costs, the uncritical adulation of the capacity of technology and the culture of Silicon Valley to change education, and a philosophy that believes in the power of number to reveal what is really transpiring in reality.[19] For students, the culture of assessment and technology makes education not a cultivation of their capacity for sympathy and empathy, but serves instead to harden them for a future life of external affirmation. The culture of assessment, bolstered by a technology that dictates how teaching and learning transpires, purifies education into a sterile exercise of mastery in critical skill sets and ways of knowing.

And when teachers do teach sympathy and empathy in their classroom, it is evaluated by some quantification metric to demonstrate students have learnt. The current culture of assessment and technology does not encourage an environment of introspection, reflection, and self-examination because the quantifiable measurement of these activities fails to reveal wholly and deeply what students experience. The Likert scale cannot capture the complexity of what transpires in the encounter between teacher and students: the teacher's content and delivery and the students' reception of it; the personalities and the particular histories of each person on that day; the specific moments of discussions, questions, and conversations; the camaraderie of partaking in a common endeavor; the tedium of fulfilling and evaluating assignments; the process of discovery, curiosity, and reflection. Because these activities and experiences do not conform to the technological design of learning and the quantifiable character of assessment, they do not count. Teachers therefore are pressured to teach in a way that steers students away from the interiority of their lives and towards a learning that can be externally sanctioned, measured, and affirmed.

Working within this culture of assessment and technology, teachers can be creative in finding ways to have students reflect upon their character, as well as to encourage them to sympathize and empathize with others unlike them. Teachers can assign content that may challenge students' sense of meritocracy by showing how chance and serendipity plays an important role in the formation and achievements of people. Certain works—like Toni Morrison's *Beloved*, J. D. Vance's *Hillbilly Elegy*, or the film, *The Kite Runner*—can provide perspectives on how other people live and what are their values in their interior lives. Teachers can tack on a qualitative assessment in their assignments to prompt students to think and reflect about what they have read. They can encourage discussion, whether in small groups, seminars, or using the Socratic Method, for students to express their view in an environment conducive to reason and civility.

Teachers can also work with other university programs to cultivate sympathy and empathy in students. For example, the invitation of a speaker from the office of diversity into the classroom can be followed by an assignment that employs reason, logic, and evidence to analyze the presentation. It would be an opportunity to teach students both a critical skill set and a different perspective that would foster their sympathy and empathy for others unlike them: What were the concerns of the speaker? Are they consistent with one another or contradictory, and how so? What evidence supports the speaker's claims? What theory or paradigm best accounts for the speaker's position? Are the solutions proposed feasible and effective or utopian and emotive? How do the speaker's experiences differ from yours, and do these differences account for your divergent opinions? What role does experience play in shaping one's way of seeing the world, and what is the role of reason in making sense of one's experience?

Special programs are also another way for teachers to develop students' sympathy and empathy: internships, study abroad, service-learning, civic engagement, and other experiences outside of the classroom are opportunities for students to be with others unlike themselves and thereby to sympathize and empathize with them.[20] However, teachers must cautious about such opportunities, knowing that the practicality of these programs is often at the cost of their academic rigor. Teachers should aim to blend both academic standards and experiential learning together in the formation of a student's intellect and sociability while, at the same time, providing assignments that prompt reflection and an active interior life.

But if teachers want to cultivate students' interior lives, they are confronted with the challenge of creating more work for themselves by adding non-quantifiable and non-technological components in their classroom. The chance to do more work without compensation hardly seems like an enticing proposition. Teachers therefore work within their universities to change how assessment is designed so that assessment is part of the classroom exercises rather than being something additional and external to it. Assessment already is taking place in the classroom, as evaluated by the students' grade. Thus, teachers should be able to use their own evaluations as the assessment of student learning rather than having something externally imposed upon them.

Another approach is to design assessment so that it is flexible enough to accommodate the variety of contents and the multiplicity of its delivery in the classroom (e.g., qualitative, quantitative, technological, and non-technological). There should not be a one-size-fits-all approach to assessment such that it drives what is being taught or how teaching transpires; instead, the assessment should be a template that permits a multitude of ways to teach and evaluate. This way the dual approach of assessment and grades as separate activities in the classroom is erased and becomes one and the same.

## The Student as Data

The credentialization of knowledge by university accreditors is one of the primary drivers in the standardization of knowledge and the growth of administrators and staff.[21] To be certified by these accreditors is to have access to the federal government's financial loans so students can borrow in order to pay for school. The traditional division of supervising universities—the federal government monitors issues of financial support and access, the states focus on consumer protection, and accreditors examine educational quality—has changed with the federal and state governments relinquishing their responsibilities to accreditors.

Accreditors now include access and consumer protection in their mission to see whether universities are ensuring equal access to all types of individuals and groups for an education and to see whether students are learning.[22] These two responsibilities are amendable to metrics of quantification by examining how students received financial support and default on their loans, how many students are retained and graduate, how many students are employed after graduation and how much they make afterwards. The outcomes especially for student learning have changed from qualitative, peer-review self-studies to corporate documents of strategic mission statements, branding, and numerical data. Universities are now accountable to these metrics with poorer outcomes interpreted as a sign of failure rather than a baseline from which the institution should improve.[23]

Quality of education consequently is defined in the metrics of student retention and postgraduate salaries rather than evaluations of student character and reflections about life. These metrics assert themselves even more today because in the age of technology information is more available. Data, as the numerical assignment and valuing of reality, has the illusion of being objective and transparent.[24] It is therefore a valuable commodity by which accreditors, administrators, teachers, and students evaluate themselves. Those experiences, activities, and moments not amendable to the pre-set standardized categories of evaluations are ignored. It is no wonder that the university is governed by the metrics of external affirmation because of the ease and attractiveness of data that accreditors use to see whether an educational institute has succeeded or failed.

The power of data resides in its apparent objectivity, an attractiveness that is especially appealing in democratic societies where, according to Tocqueville, individuals believe that everyone has an equal right to understand reality for him- or herself.[25] In democratic societies, each individual relies upon his or her own judgment to make decisions and reduces everything to its practical or utilitarian value: to "accept tradition only as a means of information, and existing facts only as lesson to be used in doing otherwise and doing better."[26] But because everyone is equal to one another in democratic society, no one is certain that his or her judgment is better than anyone else's, ultimately yielding a consensus dominated by the majority.

Data is the crystallization of democratic judgment because nobody can object to it: it is objective, transparent, and universally accessible.

Data therefore is employed to evaluate university access, faculty scholarship, student learning, and other educational functions. But the assumptions behind the creation and reception of data require examination, for data is a type of scientism, an ideology that assumes the fact-value distinction where facts are derived only from the scientific-technological method and values are products of only subjective prejudice.[27] On the one hand, knowledge is restricted to realities that conform to the scientific-technological method because this process is objective, valid, and universal; on the other hand, any reality outside of this method is an illegitimate form of knowledge because it is unscientific. The use of data by accreditors, universities, teachers, and students is to de-legitimate a whole set of experiences and knowledge that cannot be standardized or quantified in a pre-given way.

Now there is nothing wrong with data as long as it is recognized as one way of evaluation among many.[28] The problem today is that data is the only way to evaluate anything in education. This not only neglects a valuable body of knowledge and experiences, particularly those which are needed for cultivating sympathy and empathy, but it also has several potential negative consequences. Muller lists a number of these problems, such as goal displacement through diversion of effort towards what gets measured; the promotion of short-termism and the discouragement of risk-tasking and innovation; the cost in people's time to compile data; as well as diminished cooperation and common purpose in the university where reward is based on individualized measured performance.[29] Rather than cooperation and teamwork, competition and rivalry become the driving motivation for people.

The university's demand for more data also changes the nature and purpose of teaching from cultivation of the interiority of a student's intellect and character to mastery of measurable performances in skill sets. Students therefore see education as a series of competencies to be conquered before graduation and a career; teachers view their vocation in terms of citation indexes and student evaluation scores; and administrators conceive of the university as a store to placate student consumers, manage teacher employees, and appease the accreditor board.[30] The university has become like any other business in the United States governed to maximum growth, minimize liability, and motivated by profit.

There are no immediate practical solutions to this present state of American higher education. Accreditors and administrators are too entrenched in their power while students and teachers implicitly agree with this arrangement so as long as students pass their courses and teachers are mostly left alone. The university has become the preparatory grounds for students to succeed in a globalized economy where things are quantified, standardized, and externally sanctioned. The interior life of the students, their character and the cultivation of sympathy and empathy, is absent in this world because it cannot be measured.

## Student Knowledge

A broader conversation about the purpose of university education is required to shift from the paradigm of data, external affirmation, and the globalized economy to one of judgment, the interior life, and the humane world of sympathy and empathy.[31] There are some programs, colleges, and universities where this transpires, but a societal shift, if one were to occur, will take several generations and therefore calls for patience and perseverance. Nonetheless, conversations about how to transform the university can be made now, planting the seeds for a different perspective about the nature and purpose of higher education in the future.

Cases have been made about changing the university to be more aligned with the cultivation of the interior life, but they have little traction in today's public conversations. For instance, the appeals to tradition and the arguments about the inherent value of liberal education are akin to religious belief because they are only persuasive if one already agrees with them.[32] And other arguments about teaching students critical skill sets and civic engagement only reinforce the life of external affirmations.[33]

One possible way to promote cultivation of the interior life as part of the primary purpose of education is to talk about the need to develop students' prudence.[34] Adopting an Aristotelian account of prudence, I would define this excellence as both theoretical and practical reasoning that demands one be flexible in his or her pursuit of moral virtue without collapsing into cynical calculation or abstract speculation. Teaching students prudence would require the academic rigor of the classroom as well as experiential activities outside it where students learn how theoretical and practical reality intersect. Students would learn how their interior lives do not always comport with their external ones; this is not necessarily a bad thing, but a basic part of the human condition.

Such a disconnect can prompt students to reflect why this is the case and how others have confronted this situation, thereby leading them to conclude that suffering—especially recognizing and acknowledging one's own inadequacy and dependency on others—is the beginning path towards wisdom. It also would help students to see that the suffering of others, especially those who are less fortunate, is a matter of chance rather than a moral failing. To sympathize and empathize with others is to build one's interior life.

As societal institutions, universities are uniquely situated to teach students prudence. Unlike business, where theoretical reason is in the service of practical aims, or the liberal arts school, where practical reason is neglected for theory, the university can value both theoretical and practical reason equally, even when they are at times in conflict with each other.[35] By navigating between the extremes of the business and the liberal arts school, the university can teach students how to reason both theoretically and practically. Such a case about the nature and purpose of education would satisfy those who are only concerned about utility and those who only care about theory. The university fulfills both needs and, in the process, provides external and internal affirmations for students.

How a paradigm of prudence be implemented in universities would depend upon the type of institution. For example, religious institutions may focus on theological beliefs in the formation of their students, while public institutions may make civic and democratic engagement their primary mission.[36] Just as there is a diversity of universities in the United States, there is likewise a multitude of ways that prudence can be realized, as long as both theoretical and practical reason are taught. Hopefully over time accreditors would recognize that educational quality can be defined in numerous, non-numerical ways.

A paradigm of prudence provides an opportunity for universities to think about their mission, and it can serve as a unifying idea to cohere the activities of teaching, scholarship, and service. It forces universities to determine the proper balance between theoretical and practical reasoning in its curriculum for students, the type of scholarship it wants its faculty to produce, and the kind of service it wants its members to engage. The paradigm of prudence makes possible this type of conversation within the university and demonstrates its value to the public. It may not stop today's questioning of the value of the American university but it at least offers a response that allows the cultivation of the interior lives of students while, at the same, providing them with opportunities for external affirmation.[37]

The character of today's student, the power of accreditors, and the predominance of data metrics have yielded a world where the cultivation and expression of the interior life is seen as a sign of personal weakness and moral failing. To be vulnerable, exposed, and unguarded; to admit one's own inadequacies and dependency upon others; and to empathize with those less fortunate are experiences and expressions that resist quantification and standardization and therefore are not encouraged, unless for ideological reasons of diversity or the reinforcement of belief in one's own meritocratic superiority. Students today do not want to suffer—they do not want to sympathize and empathize in a genuine and humane way—and so they pursue a career defined by the external affirmations of money, status, and power; in turn, they are less able to reflect upon the meaning of life or to care for others, refusing to be open to the messiness of life, with all its glory and horror.

## Notes

1. I would like to thank Richard Avramenko, the Center for the Study of Liberal Democracy at the University of Wisconsin–Madison, and Saginaw Valley State University for supporting my sabbatical which enabled me to write this chapter.
2. This characterization does not apply to all American college students but, as we will see below, it is a reflection of what is occurring on most college campuses today.
3. W. Deresiewicz, *Excellent Sheep: The Miseducation of the American Elite and the Way to a Meaningful Life* (New York: Free Press, 2014). For a view that disagrees, see D. Bok, *Our Underachieving Colleges: A Candid Look at How Much Students Learn and Why They Should Be Learning More* (Princeton: Princeton University Press, 2006); R. Arum and J. Roksa *Academically Adrift: Limited Learning on College Campuses* (Chicago: University of Chicago Press, 2011).
4. F. Furedi, *What's Happened to the University? A Sociological Exploration of Its Infanilisation* (New York: Routledge, 2016); M. Rectenwalk, *Springtime for Snowflakes: "Social Justice" and Its Postmodern Parentage* (Nashville, TN: New England Review Press, 2018).
5. D. Brooks, "The Organizational Kid," *The Atlantic*, April 2001. Available at https://www.theatlantic.com/magazine/archive/2001/04/the-organization-kid/302164/.

6. R. Srigley, "Dear Parents: Everything You Need to Know About Your Son's and Daughter's University but Don't," *Los Angeles Review of Books*, December 9, 2015. Available at https://lareviewofbooks.org/article/dear-parents-everything-you-need-to-know-about-your-son-and-daughters-university-but-dont/; G. Lukianoff and J. Haidt, *The Coddling of the American Mind: How Good Intentions and Bad Ideas Are Setting Up a Generation for Failure* (New York: Penguin, 2018); and B. Denizet-Lewis, "Why Are More American Teenagers Than Ever Suffering from Severe Anxiety," *New York Times*, October 11, 2017. Available at https://www.nytimes.com/2017/10/11/magazine/why-are-more-american-teenagers-than-ever-suffering-from-severe-anxiety.html.
7. D. Brook, *The Trap: Selling Out to Stay Afloat in Winner-Take-All-America* (New York: Times Books, 2007); F. Furedi, *What's Happened to the University?* (2016); and M. Rectenwalk, *Springtime for Snowflakes* (2018).
8. W. B. Michaels, *The Trouble with Diversity: How We Learned to Love Identity and Ignore Inequality* (Dallas: Metropolitan, 2006); J. H. McWhorter, "Closed Minds on Campus," *Wall Street Journal*, November 27, 2015. Available at https://www.wsj.com/articles/closed-minds-on-campus-1448634626; F. Furedi, *What's Happened to the University?* (2016); B. Ginsberg, "The Unholy Alliance of College Administrators and Left-Liberal Activists," *Modern Age* 59, no. 3 (2017): 17–27; M. Bauerlin, "The Bad Faith of the Professors," *Modern Age* 59, no. 3 (2017): 49–60; and M. Rectenwalk, *Springtime for Snowflakes* (2018).
9. P. Wood, "Libertarian vs. Progressives: The New Campus Divide," *Minding the Campus: Reforming Our University*, November 30, 2014. Available at https://www.mindingthecampus.org/2014/11/30/libertarians-vs-progressives-the-new-campus-divide/; W. Egginton, *The Splintering of the American Mind: Identity Politics, Inequality, and Community on Today's College Campuses* (London: Bloomsbury, 2018).
10. D. Hess, *Controversy in the Classroom: The Democratic Power of Discussion* (New York: Routledge, 2009); D. E. Hess and P. McAvoy, *The Political Classroom: Evidence and Ethics in Democratic Education* (New York: Routledge, 2015); L. Trepanier, *The Socratic Method Today: Student-Centered and Transformative Teaching in Political Science* (New York: Routledge, 2017); and S. Yaylaci and E. Beauvais, "The Role of Social Group Membership on Classroom Participation," *PS: Political Science & Politics* 50, no. 2 (2017): 559–64.
11. Specific examples can be found in and J. von Heyking and L. Trepanier, *Teaching in an Age of Ideology* (Lanham, MD: Lexington Books, 2012);

L. Trepanier, *The Liberal Arts in America* (Cedar City, UT: Southern Utah University Press, 2012).
12. D. Bok, *Universities in the Marketplace: The Commercialization of Higher Education* (Princeton: Princeton University Press, 2003); C. Newfield, *The Great Mistake: How We Wrecked Public Universities and How We Can Fix Them* (Baltimore: John Hopkins University Press, 2016); and L. Bunce, A. Baird, and S. E. Jones, "The Student-as-Consumer Approach in Higher Education and Its Effect on Academic Performance," *Studies in Higher Education* 40, no. 11 (2017): 1958–78.
13. B. Ansell and J. Gingrich, "Mismatch: University's Education and Labor Market Institutions," *PS: Political Science & Politics* 50, no. 2 (2017): 423–25; L. Graf and J. W. Powell, "How Employer Interests and Investments Shape Advanced Skill Formation," *PS: Political Science & Politics* 50, no. 2 (2017): 418–22.
14. W. Zumeta, D. W. Brenman, P. M. Callahn, and J. E. Finney, *Financing American Higher Education in the Era of Globalization* (Cambridge, MA: Harvard Education Press, 2012); J. Best and E. Best, *The Student Loan Mess: How Good Intentions Created a Trillion-Dollar Problem* (Berkeley: University of California Press, 2014); and C. Eaton, "Still Public: State Universities and America's New Student-Debt Coalitions," *PS: Political Science & Politics* 50, no. 2 (2017): 408–12.
15. L. Trepanier, *Why the Humanities Matter Today: In Defense of Liberal Education* (Lanham, MD: Lexington Books, 2017).
16. J. Palfrey and U. Gasser, *Born Digital: Understanding the First Generation of Digital Natives* (New York: Basic Books, 2008); L. Trepanier, *Technology, Science, and Democracy* (Cedar City, UT: Southern Utah University Press, 2008).
17. L. Suskie, "Why Are We Assessing?," *Inside Higher Ed*, October 26, 2010. Available at https://www.insidehighered.com/views/2010/10/26/why-are-we-assessing.
18. R. M. Palloff and K. Pratt, *Excellent Online Instructor Strategies for Professional Development* (Hoboken, NJ: Wiley, 2011).
19. A. Hacker and C. Dreifu, *Higher Education? How Colleges Are Wasting Our Money and Failing Our Kids—And What We Can Do About* (New York: Times Book, 2010); N. S. Riley, *The Faculty Lounges, and Other Reasons, Why You Won't Get the College Education You Paid for* (Lanham, MD: Ivan R. Dee, 2011); M. C. Taylor, *Crisis on Campus: A Bold Plan for Reforming Our Colleges and Universities* (New York: Kopf, 2010); W. Zumeta, *Financing American Higher Education in the Era of Globalization* (2012); J. Best, *The Student Loan Mess* (2014); S. R. Gallagher, *The Future of University Credentials: New Development at the Intersection of Higher Education and Hiring* (Cambridge, MA: Harvard

University Press, 2016); B. Caplan, *The Case Against Education: Why the Education System Is a Waste of Time and Money* (Princeton: Princeton University Press, 2018); R. Kelchen, *Higher Education Accountability* (Baltimore: John Hopkins University Press, 2018); and S. D. Phillips and K. Kisner, eds., *Accreditation on the Edge: Challenging Quality Assurance in Higher Education* (Baltimore: John Hopkins University Press, 2018).
20. R. Zemsky, G. R. Wegner, and A. J. Duffield, *Making Sense of the College Curriculum: Faculty Stories, Conflict, and Accommodation* (New Brunswick, NJ: Rutgers University Press, 2018).
21. R. Kelchen, *Higher Education Accountability* (2018); S. D. Phillips, *Accreditation on the Edge* (2018).
22. S. R. Gallagher, *The Future of University Credentials* (2016).
23. J. Z. Muller, *The Tyranny of Metrics* (Princeton: Princeton University Press, 2018), 67–88.
24. L. Floridi, *The 4th Revolution: How the Infosphere Is Reshaping Human Reality* (Oxford: Oxford University Press, 2014); D. Beer, *Metric Power* (New York: Palgrave Macmillan, 2016); and C. N. Davidson, *The New Education: How to Revolutionize the University to Prepare Students for a World in Flux* (New York: Basic Books, 2017).
25. L. Trepanier, "Tocqueville, Weber, and Democracy: The Condition of Equality and the Possibility of Charisma in America," in *Political Rhetoric and Leadership in Democracy*, ed. L. Trepanier (Cedar City, UT: Southern Utah University Press, 2011), 22–48.
26. A. de Tocqueville, *Democracy in America, Volume 2*, trans. Phillips Bradley (New York: Vintage Classics, 1990), 3.
27. L. Trepanier, "The Recovery of Science in Eric Voegelin's Thought," in *Technology, Science, and Democracy*, ed. L. Trepanier (Cedar City, UT: Southern Utah University Press, 2008), 44–54.
28. Muller provides a checklist to see whether one should use data and how to use it to evaluate performance. The checklist includes questions like "What kind of data are you thinking of measuring?", "How useful is the data?", "How useful is more data?", "What are the costs of not relying upon data?", "To what purposes will data be put: to whom will the information be made transparent?", "What are the costs of acquiring the data?", and "How and by whom is data developed?" Muller warns that even the best data are subject to corruption or goal displacement and that "recognizing the limits of the possible is the beginning of wisdom" (182). See J. Z. Mueller, *The Tyranny of Metrics*, 175–83.
29. Ibid., 169–74.
30. B. Ginsberg, *The Fall of Faculty: The Rise of the All-Administrative University and Why It Matters* (Oxford: Oxford University Press, 2011); W. G. Bowen and E. M. Tobin, *Locus of Authority: The Evolution*

*of Faculty Roles in the Governance of Higher Education* (Princeton: Princeton University Press, 2015); T. Kaufman-Osborn, "Disenchanted Professionals: The Politics of Faculty Governance in the Neoliberal Academy," *Perspectives on Politics* 15, no. 1 (2017): 100–15; and R. Srigley, "Whose University Is It Anyway?," *Los Angeles Review of Books*, February 22, 2018. Available at https://lareviewofbooks.org/article/whose-university-is-it-anyway/#!.

31. For more about the history of higher education in the United States, see P. H. Mattingly, *America Academic Cultures: A History of Higher Education* (Chicago: University of Chicago Press, 2017); see L. Trepanier, "A Philosophy of Prudence and the Purpose of Higher Education Today," in *The Relevance of Higher Education*, ed. T. Simpson (Lanham, MD: Lexington Books, 2013), 1–23.

32. J. O. Freedman, *Liberal Education and the Public Interest* (Iowa, IA: University of Iowa Press, 2003); M. Nussbaum, *Cultivating Humanities: A Classical Defense of Reform in Liberal Education* (Cambridge, MA: Harvard University Press, 1997) and *Not for Profit: Why Democracy Needs the Humanities* (Princeton: Princeton University Press, 2010); D. N. Levine *Powers of the Mind: The Reinvention of Liberal Learning in America* (Chicago: University of Chicago Press, 2006); A. Kronman, *Education's End: Why Our Colleges and Universities Have Given Up on the Meaning of Life* (New Haven: Yale University Press, 2008); M. W. Roche, *Why Choose the Liberal Arts* (Notre Dame: University of Notre Dame, 2010); and L. Trepanier, *The Democratic Discourse of Liberal Education* (Cedar City, UT: Southern Utah University Press, 2009).

33. M. Spelling, *A Test of Leadership: Charting the Future of U.S. Higher Education* (Washington, DC: U.S. Department of Education, 2006). Available at http://www2.ed.gov/about/bdscomm/list/hiedfuture/reports/pre-pub-report.pdf; B. Ansell, "Mismatch: University's Education and Labor Market Institutions" (2017); and L. Graf, "How Employer Interests and Investments Shape Advanced Skill Formation" (2017).

34. For more about this paradigm, Aristotle's definition of prudence, and how to implement in the university, see L. Trepanier, "A Philosophy of Prudence and the Purpose of Higher Education Today" (2013).

35. L. Trepanier, "A Philosophy of Prudence and the Purpose of Higher Education Today" (2013).

36. G. Moreno-Riano, P. Hamilton, and L. Trepanier, "Statesmanship and Democracy in a Global and Comparative Context," in *The Liberal Arts in America*, ed. L. Trepanier (Cedar City, UT: Southern Utah University Press, 2012), 128–48 and "Teaching the American Political Tradition

in a Global Context," in *The Liberal Arts in America*, ed. L. Trepanier (Cedar City, UT: Southern Utah University Press, 2012), 149–66.
37. Some recent examples of criticism of the university are A. Hacker, *Higher Education?* (2010); N. S. Riley, *The Faculty Lounges* (2011); M. C. Taylor, *Crisis on Campus* (2010); and B. Caplan, *The Case Against Education: Why the Education System Is a Waste of Time and Money* (Princeton: Princeton University Press, 2018).

## References

Ansell, B. and J. Gingrich. "Mismatch: University's Education and Labor Market Institutions." *PS: Political Science & Politics* 50, no. 2 (2017): 423–25.
Arum, R. and J. Roksa. *Academically Adrift: Limited Learning on College Campuses*. Chicago: University of Chicago Press, 2011.
Bauerlin, M. "The Bad Faith of the Professors." *Modern Age* 59, no. 3 (2017): 49–60.
Beer, D. *Metric Power*. New York: Palgrave Macmillan, 2016.
Best, J. and E. Best. *The Student Loan Mess: How Good Intentions Created a Trillion-Dollar Problem*. Berkeley: University of California Press, 2014.
Bok, D. *Universities in the Marketplace: The Commercialization of Higher Education*. Princeton: Princeton University Press, 2003.
Bok, D. *Our Underachieving Colleges: A Candid Look at How Much Students Learn and Why They Should Be Learning More*. Princeton: Princeton University Press, 2006.
Bowen, W. G. and E. M. Tobin. *Locus of Authority: The Evolution of Faculty Roles in the Governance of Higher Education*. Princeton: Princeton University Press, 2015.
Brooks, D. "The Organizational Kid." *The Atlantic*, April 2001. Available at https://www.theatlantic.com/magazine/archive/2001/04/the-organization-kid/302164/.
Brook, D. *The Trap: Selling Out to Stay Afloat in Winner-Take-All-America*. New York: Times Books, 2007.
Bunce, L., A. Baird, and S. E. Jones. "The Student-as-Consumer Approach in Higher Education and Its Effect on Academic Performance." *Studies in Higher Education* 40, no. 11 (2017): 1958–78.
Caplan, B. *The Case Against Education: Why the Education System Is a Waste of Time and Money*. Princeton: Princeton University Press, 2018.
Davidson, C. N. *The New Education: How to Revolutionize the University to Prepare Students for a World in Flux*. New York: Basic Books, 2017.
Deresiewicz, W. *Excellent Sheep: The Miseducation of the American Elite and the Way to a Meaningful Life*. New York: Free Press, 2014.

Eaton, C. "Still Public: State Universities and America's New Student-Debt Coalitions." *PS: Political Science & Politics* 50, no. 2 (2017): 408–12.

Egginton, W. *The Splintering of the American Mind: Identity Politics, Inequality, and Community on Today's College Campuses.* London: Bloomsbury, 2018.

Floridi, L. *The 4th Revolution: How the Infosphere Is Reshaping Human Reality.* Oxford: Oxford University Press, 2014.

Freedman, J. O. *Liberal Education and the Public Interest.* Iowa, IA: University of Iowa Press, 2003.

Furedi, F. *What's Happened to the University? A Sociological Exploration of Its Infanilisation.* New York: Routledge, 2016.

Gallagher, S. R. *The Future of University Credentials: New Development at the Intersection of Higher Education and Hiring.* Cambridge, MA: Harvard University Press, 2016.

Ginsberg, B. *The Fall of Faculty: The Rise of the All-Administrative University and Why It Matters.* Oxford: Oxford University Press, 2011.

Ginsberg, B. "The Unholy Alliance of College Administrators and Left-Liberal Activists." *Modern Age* 59, no. 3 (2017): 17–27.

Graf, L. and J. W. Powell. "How Employer Interests and Investments Shape Advanced Skill Formation." *PS: Political Science & Politics* 50, no. 2 (2017): 418–22.

Hacker, A. and C. Dreifu. *Higher Education? How Colleges Are Wasting Our Money and Failing Our Kids—And What We Can Do About.* New York: Times Books, 2010.

Hess, D. E. *Controversy in the Classroom: The Democratic Power of Discussion.* New York: Routledge, 2009.

Hess, D. E. and P. McAvoy. *The Political Classroom: Evidence and Ethics in Democratic Education.* New York: Routledge, 2015.

von Heyking, J. and L. Trepanier. *Teaching in an Age of Ideology.* Lanham, MD: Lexington Books, 2012.

Kaufman-Osborn, T. "Disenchanted Professionals: The Politics of Faculty Governance in the Neoliberal Academy." *Perspectives on Politics* 15, no. 1 (2017): 100–15.

Kelchen, R. *Higher Education Accountability.* Baltimore: John Hopkins University Press, 2018.

Kronman, A. *Education's End: Why Our Colleges and Universities Have Given Up on the Meaning of Life.* New Haven: Yale University Press, 2008.

Levine, D. N. *Powers of the Mind: The Reinvention of Liberal Learning in America.* Chicago: University of Chicago Press, 2006.

Lukianoff, G. and J. Haidt. *The Coddling of the American Mind: How Good Intentions and Bad Ideas Are Setting Up a Generation for Failure.* New York: Penguin Books, 2018.

Mattingly, P. H. *America Academic Cultures: A History of Higher Education*. Chicago: University of Chicago Press, 2017.
McWhorter, J. H. "Closed Minds on Campus." *Wall Street Journal*, November 27, 2015. Available at https://www.wsj.com/articles/closed-minds-on-campus-1448634626.
Michaels, W. B. *The Trouble with Diversity: How We Learned to Love Identity and Ignore Inequality*. Dallas: Metropolitan, 2006.
Moreno-Riano, G., P. Hamilton, and L. Trepanier. "Statesmanship and Democracy in a Global and Comparative Context." In *The Liberal Arts in America*, ed. L. Trepanier. Cedar City, UT: Southern Utah University Press, 2012a: 128–48.
Moreno-Riano, G., P. Hamilton, and L. Trepanier. "Teaching the American Political Tradition in a Global Context." In *The Liberal Arts in America*, ed. L. Trepanier. Cedar City, UT: Southern Utah University Press, 2012b: 149–66.
Muller, J. Z. *The Tyranny of Metrics*. Princeton: Princeton University Press, 2018.
Newfield, C. *The Great Mistake: How We Wrecked Public Universities and How We Can Fix Them*. Baltimore: John Hopkins University Press, 2016.
Nussbaum, M. *Cultivating Humanities: A Classical Defense of Reform in Liberal Education*. Cambridge, MA: Harvard University Press, 1997.
Nussbaum, M. *Not for Profit: Why Democracy Needs the Humanities*. Princeton: Princeton University Press, 2010.
Palfrey, J. and U. Gasser. *Born Digital: Understanding the First Generation of Digital Natives*. New York: Basic Books, 2008.
Palloff, R. M. and K. Pratt. *Excellent Online Instructor Strategies for Professional Development*. Hoboken, NJ: Wiley, 2011.
Phillips, S. D. and K. Kisner, eds. *Accreditation on the Edge: Challenging Quality Assurance in Higher Education*. Baltimore: John Hopkins University Press, 2018.
Rectenwalk, M. *Springtime for Snowflakes: "Social Justice" and Its Postmodern Parentage*. Nashville, TN: New England Review Press, 2018.
Riley, N. S. *The Faculty Lounges, and Other Reasons, Why You Won't Get the College Education You Paid For*. Lanham, MD: Ivan R. Dee, 2011.
Roche, M. W. *Why Choose the Liberal Arts*. Notre Dame: University of Notre Dame, 2010.
Rose, D. "Higher Education and the Transformation of American Citizenship." *PS: Political Science & Politics* 50, no. 2 (2017): 403–7.
Spelling, M. *A Test of Leadership: Charting the Future of U.S. Higher Education*. Washington, DC: U.S. Department of Education, 2006. Available at http://www2.ed.gov/about/bdscomm/list/hiedfuture/reports/pre-pub-report.pdf.

Srigley, R. "Dear Parents: Everything You Need to Know About Your Son's and Daughter's University but Don't." *Los Angeles Review of Books*, December 9, 2015. Available at https://lareviewofbooks.org/article/dear-parents-everything-you-need-to-know-about-your-son-and-daughters-university-but-dont/.

Srigley, R. "Whose University Is It Anyway?" *Los Angeles Review of Books*, February 22, 2018. Available at https://lareviewofbooks.org/article/whose-university-is-it-anyway/#!.

Suskie, L. "Why Are We Assessing?" *Inside Higher Ed*, October 26, 2010. Available at https://www.insidehighered.com/views/2010/10/26/why-are-we-assessing.

Taylor, M. C. *Crisis on Campus: A Bold Plan for Reforming Our Colleges and Universities*. New York: Kopf, 2010.

Tocqueville, A. *Democracy in America, Volume 2*. Trans. Phillips Bradley. New York: Vintage Classics, 1990.

Trepanier, L. *Technology, Science, and Democracy*. Cedar City, UT: Southern Utah University Press, 2008a.

Trepanier, L. "The Recovery of Science in Eric Voegelin's Thought." In *Technology, Science, and Democracy*, ed. L. Trepanier. Cedar City, UT: Southern Utah University Press, 2008b: 44–54.

Trepanier, L. *The Democratic Discourse of Liberal Education*. Cedar City, UT: Southern Utah University Press, 2009.

Trepanier, L. "Tocqueville, Weber, and Democracy: The Condition of Equality and the Possibility of Charisma in America." In *Political Rhetoric and Leadership in Democracy*, ed. L. Trepanier. Cedar City, UT: Southern Utah University Press, 2011: 22–48.

Trepanier, L. *The Liberal Arts in America*. Cedar City, UT: Southern Utah University Press, 2012.

Trepanier, L. "A Philosophy of Prudence and the Purpose of Higher Education Today." In *The Relevance of Higher Education*, ed. T. Simpson. Lanham, MD: Lexington Books, 2013: 1–23.

Trepanier, L. *Why the Humanities Matter Today: In Defense of Liberal Education*. Lanham, MD: Lexington Books, 2017a.

Trepanier, L. *The Socratic Method Today: Student-Centered and Transformative Teaching in Political Science*. New York: Routledge, 2017b.

Wood, P. "Libertarian vs. Progressives: The New Campus Divide." In *Minding the Campus: Reforming Our University*, November 30, 2014. Available at https://www.mindingthecampus.org/2014/11/30/libertarians-vs-progressives-the-new-campus-divide/.

Yaylaci, S. and E. Beauvais. "The Role of Social Group Membership on Classroom Participation." *PS: Political Science & Politics* 50, no. 2 (2017): 559–64.

Zemsky, R., G. R. Wegner, and A. J. Duffield. *Making Sense of the College Curriculum: Faculty Stories, Conflict, and Accommodation.* New Brunswick, NJ: Rutgers University Press, 2018.

Zumeta, W., D. W. Brenman, P. M. Callahn, and J. E. Finney. *Financing American Higher Education in the Era of Globalization.* Cambridge, MA: Harvard Education Press, 2012.

# The Drawing Lesson

*Kelley Aitken*

First things first, I say, you've got to
organize the page and establish where
the shapes are in space. We're astronomers,
these pencils our telescopes, her face a distant
constellation. Show us, they say as I loop ovals
across white paper. It's not about getting it
perfectly but getting it down, honing happens
later, these are approximations or approaches,
birds in flight that will eventually land, which,
according to their frowns, is a load of claptrap.

So I talk planes, saying everything is faceted,
the face a soft diamond. Their temples flutter
with exasperation, their hands with mild panic
and *I don't understand* snaps like an elastic
at the soft inner wrist of my patience.

"Can I touch your face?"

I press that cliff wall of understanding,
cheek and brow into which I'd push
a geology of drawing. Concavity, I say,
and protrusion; it's all planar. Three fingers
lifted, shifted, placed against cartilage,
muscle, the gentle upholstery of flesh. See?
But what I really mean is: Feel?
Your face, facing so many directions.

They've got the goon show going,
malformed potatoes, eggs wearing
wigs, Nefertiti's neck, their drawings
are *hydrocephalic* and

                      in a flash I'm back at crip-camp, London,
                      Ontario, and my beginnings as an art teacher:
                      With every busload I'd hide in the arts-and-
                      crafts cabin while they sang, "There might be
                      flies on some of you guys but there ain't no
                      flies on us." Half of them no longer alive for
                      me to draw their wonky bravery. By the time
                      they got back on the bus I saw their massive
                      skulls and sloppy grins as just another
                      manifestation of the body's wide diversity.
                      We were all weightless in that pool.

Now I'm talking shade and light, the
particularities of downy warmth or shine,
the grease of the face, its bacon and grist,
bumps, knobs, follicles, stray hairs, eyebrows
like Nike slogans or wheat fields, the sag
where skin, fatigued, no longer resists
the planetary pull *but you can't use line*
because it adds a decade. Areas of tone
will bring this forth out of nothing, like
we were brought, once.

I'm using words, the grand
obfuscators, to make form clear. Drawing
is about looking, I say, for the umpteenth
time. Put down what you see and check what
you've put down against what you see but
maybe too much of life is measuring. We
press on, fingers to cheek and pencil
to page, coming away from these
nights like wet noodles because I
persist in pulling, from them, such
scrutiny as we so rarely offer or receive.

Our eyes on the beautiful Tati, our hands
around pencils with rounded tips. In
cross-hatched mass and smudge, some
vestige of spirit catches. Decades later,
whoever looks at these will see her
as we do, tonight.

# Chapter 16:
# A Time to Weep and a Time to Laugh, Or, the Necessity of Suffering Even As We Live Happily Ever After

*Dorothy Warner*

Nations that lose, in a single year, thousands (in the case of Canada) or tens of thousands (in the case of the United States) of their citizens to drug overdose or suicide are nations with many citizens ill equipped to handle suffering. While this effect may seem a matter of public health, there is no policy, no decree, no amount of taxation or spending, that can teach individual persons to bear suffering. That kind of instruction best comes from families and, to a certain extent, educators. Consider the attitudes towards human suffering offered to us in the following three sources. First, the words of Qoheleth situate our wondering about the meaning of why we must suffer in a broader, trans-historical context:

---

D. Warner (✉)
Writer and Former Educator, Washington, DC, USA

© The Author(s) 2019
S. Steel and A. Homeniuk (eds.),
*Suffering and the Intelligence of Love in the Teaching Life*,
https://doi.org/10.1007/978-3-030-05958-3_24

> There is a time for everything,
> and a season for every activity under the heavens...
> a time to weep and a time to laugh,
> a time to mourn and a time to dance,
> a time to scatter stones and a time to gather them,
> a time to embrace and a time to refrain from embracing.[1]

Second, William Hill would have us develop our understanding of suffering in terms of its relation to the transformative power of love when he writes:

> You've got to give a little, take a little, And let your poor heart break a little. That's the story of, that's the glory of love. You've got to laugh a little, cry a little, Until the clouds roll by a little. That's the story of, that's the glory of love.[2]

Finally, C. S. Lewis gives us pause when we, naturally enough, castigate and vilify the role of pain and suffering in our lives:

> The tendency of this or that novelist or poet may represent suffering as wholly bad in its effects, as producing, and justifying, every kind of malice and brutality in the sufferer. And, of course, pain, like pleasure, can be so received: all that is given to a creature with free will must be two-edged, not by the nature of the giver or of the gift, but by the nature of the recipient. And, again, the evil results of pain can be multiplied if sufferers are persistently taught by the bystanders that such results are the proper and manly results for them to exhibit...But I am not convinced that suffering, if spared such officious vicarious indignation, has any natural tendency to produce such evils.[3]

When we consent to marriage and family, we open ourselves to the joys and sorrows of those whom we love. Viewing love as an activity, there are actions we take to relieve the suffering of those around us, and actions others take to relieve ours. It sometimes happens that family members are inadequate to those tasks; that, too, becomes part of our own suffering, but through any suffering, we have the opportunity to grow in love. Blessedly, family life does not occur in a vacuum, and we can turn in some times of trial to friends, community, and institutions that can mitigate suffering in ways that complement the role of the family.

Every doctor, nurse, and parent present at the delivery of a new baby waits for this—the child's first cry. Which is to say, that for every single human being, as far as we can tell, the first moment of life is one of suffering. For almost all of us, there is a mother, and for most of us, also a father, there, to help us through that first moment, and many moments to follow, when, audibly or inaudibly, loudly or softly, we cry out from suffering caused by hunger, thirst, discomfort, pain, sorrow. Notwithstanding that first, universal experience, our contemporary culture seems perplexed by suffering. While there is more and more talk of "trauma" in the experiences of our children, there is nevertheless little offered to the children who endure those traumas, beyond therapeutic or pharmaceutical remedies. If suffering is inevitable, should we not do our best to provide, from a child's early days, psychological resilience to what will surely come to each of us? We have, in the human experience, a valuable tool to build resilience to suffering—that tool is the family.

When couples begin their lives together, there is little talk of suffering. Who would download a dating app that asked, "How do you react to news of a death in your family?" or "What would you do if you were presented a diagnosis of a terminal illness?" Such questions are crowded out by queries regarding travel, food, (possibly) religion, ethnicity, movies, and so on. But one might argue that the first kinds of questions are more to the heart, so to say, of what a long-lasting relationship will need to endure.

The problem is compounded by our modern tendency to remove those who are suffering from the public eye. The frail elderly opt for, or are opted into, assisted living; the preborn are tested for diseases that may disqualify them from ever uttering that newborn cry; the terminally ill are offered hospice care. To be sure, the poor are always with us—no nation is without its beggars and indigent, no matter whether they are called homeless or gypsies. But it falls upon most of us, in the developed world, to seek out the sick, the poor, the lonely, the dying—they may be hidden from our daily lives.

And yet, that helpless child's first cry is a sign that a human infant will require years of concentrated care, and still more years of serious attention, before an independent adult emerges. Family life is a child's primary and most enduring educational experience. No formal schooling will override the negative or positive lessons a child learns from family life. Whether recognized or not, part of a complete family experience is the experience of suffering. Strong families "laugh a little" but also "cry a little." A family that can process and endure suffering, loss, sorrow, and, yes, trauma, will carry that strength into happier times, as well.

Some families have suffering thrust upon them. A few examples come quickly to mind: a newly married couple who left their wedding reception following an ambulance, in which rode the father of bride, who would die later that day; a couple whose first child died during what was promised to be a routine labor and delivery; another who planned their wedding around the young groom's cancer treatments; military couples who face deployments and the associated uncertainties. These kinds of couples are tested and proven, early on—whatever comes later, having come through those trials, they have a background of steadfastness in adversity. Should families, then, wish for suffering? Perhaps not; but there are ways to offer to share the sufferings of others, and those offerings may help us build our family's strengths for future trials.

From their very early years, children who learn the discipline of family life are better equipped to endure life's discomforts. Families that serve meals at regular times teach children to experience an hour's worth of hunger. Hosting a gathering, even a very simple one, teaches the small sacrifices made so that guests are made comfortable. Small, recurring traditions—a special meal, a favorite place to walk, a shared book—can build security and provide comfort. These ordinary activities show children a united sense of family purpose and can help serve as a framework to absorb more serious sufferings. The goal is to foster resilience for the family as a whole, and for each of its members.

As families mature, there are three chief ways they can educate their children in resilience. Firstly, children can be reminded of the sufferings of those around them, whether visible or invisible. Sickness in one family member may serve as an occasion for a child to assist the sick person (perhaps if only by playing more quietly). Extended family members, or family friends, who are in hospitals or in nursing care, may be visited, or called, or sent messages, small gifts or cards. Secondly, children can be taught, by example and instruction, to bear small sufferings patiently. Can a minor injury be sustained with a minimum of tears? Can hunger or thirst be borne until meal or snack time? Thirdly, children can be shown how to take on small sufferings—in some families these are called "chores"—for the good of the whole.

Strong families are made stronger by friendship. It is cliched but bears repeating: the ties of friendship are the most valuable assets we have. The moral, spiritual, and in some cases physical supports offered through friendship cannot be purchased at any price and yet are vital to providing the necessary cushions we will all need, at one time or another, as life brings us its low moments. As family members support each other, so a web of friends supports the family.

Teachers might well contemplate this question: would they prefer students who are resilient to those who are fragile? If the former, there are classroom lessons in resilience, as well. As with families, classes may "adopt" elderly or institutionalized individuals for visits or other contacts; class expectations regarding small injuries, whether physical or social, can be enforced; and classes, like families, can have designated chores and responsibilities. Most teachers cannot choose the family background of their students, but they can reinforce, or, in some cases, introduce, lessons of resilience through the content of instruction. History lessons can include figures such as Abraham Lincoln, who, reflecting on his mother's death when he was a boy, wrote to Fanny McCullough: "In this sad world of ours, sorrow comes to all; and, to the young, it comes with bitterest agony; because it takes them unawares ... I have had experience enough to know what I say."[4] Contemporary authors such as J. D. Vance (*Hillbilly Elegy*) and Bei Dao (*City Gate, Open Up*) offer poignant examples of resilience developed through family experience even under the extreme strains of drug addiction, violence, and political repression. The old film line about how "the problems of three little people don't amount to a hill of beans" against the larger upheavals of a world war, carries a kind of wisdom: all of us need to learn the difference between our own "hill of beans" and problems that truly deserve attention and sympathy.[5] To that end, the classroom can be a place where lessons on geography include, as appropriate, instruction in how the world's peoples live, some with great suffering, on a daily basis. These lessons do not of themselves diminish whatever sufferings the students may be bearing, but they may provide perspective. As with family life, the community of the classroom is also enriched and supported by friendships, between and among the students, teachers, and staff.

We must acknowledge that certain sufferings arise within the family—whether through ordinary tensions and trials, or through abuse, neglect, or family breakdown. Here is where an educator may feel the most powerless but may also have the most influence. Anyone who has come from a difficult family background and gone on to be successful has a mentor, often a teacher, to thank. For inspiration, one might suggest a look at the team members profiled in Daniel James Brown's *The Boys in the Boat*, who faced significant family and economic challenges on their way to an Olympic medal.

Resilience learned in one family can be passed, generationally, to the next. Consider author Devin Foley, whose chronic physical pain has brought him to the brink of despair. And yet he writes:

> I have a beautiful wife and six incredible children. I love them with all my being. They are second only to my love of the Creator. My father died when I was a child. As such, I know how difficult it is for a single mom and fatherless children. I have a duty to live for God and for my family. When it comes to those darkest of times, it is as simple as that. My affliction, my pain, does not excuse me from my roles as husband and father. My family's love helps sustain me, and I hope that my love and sacrifice will help sustain them.[6]

We have no reason to expect that human suffering will go away. Technology can, in some times and places, relieve it, but a moment's reflection reminds us that technology has also made monumental contributions to human suffering. Likewise, while there may be times and places when a legal remedy is in order as a way to enforce a just punishment on an offender, that legal remedy will not *ipso facto* take away the suffering. Nor does financial or social success remove the possibility of suffering. The American entertainer Carol Burnett's daughter abused drugs as a teenager. Burnett recalled, "I put her in a third rehab place, and oh my God, she hated me. I came to the conclusion that I had to love her enough to let her hate me. She got sober and we started bonding. We wound up working together, writing a play together." When her daughter died from cancer, Burnett commented, "You don't get over it, but you cope. What else can you do?"[7] Country singer Willie Nelson used a family tragedy as inspiration for his song with the line, "It's not somethin' you get over, But it's somethin' you get through."[8] It is perhaps the most fundamental role of the family to show each member how to "get through" the sufferings and sorrows that we will each experience.

## NOTES

1. *Ecclesiastes* 3: 1, 4–5.
2. William Hill, *The Glory of Love* (song lyrics) 1936.
3. C. S. Lewis, "The Problem of Pain," in *The Complete C. S. Lewis* (San Francisco: Harper, 2002), 613.
4. Abraham Lincoln, "Letter to Fanny McCullough," in *The Collected Works of Abraham Lincoln* (Rutgers University Press, 1955), 15–16.
5. *Casablanca*, directed by Michael Curtiz (1942; Warner Bros. Pictures).
6. Devon Foley, "Suicide: I've Heard Its Siren Call," *Intellectual Takeout: A Refuge for Rational Discourse*, June 11, 2018. http://www.intellectualtakeout.org/article/suicide-ive-heard-its-siren-call.
7. J. D. Heyman and Gillian Telling. "Carol Burnett, 85, Opens Up About Her Daughter's Tragic Death: I Think About Her Every Day," May 2, 2018. https://people.com/tv/carol-burnett-daughter-tragic-death/.
8. Willie Nelson, "Something You Get Through," released April 6, 2018, track 5 on *Last Man Standing*. Sound Emporium Studios, Legacy Recording.

## REFERENCES

Brown, Daniel James. *The Boys in the Boat*. London: Penguin, 2013.
Curtiz, Michael, dir. *Casablanca*. Warner Bros. Pictures, 1942.
Dao, Bei. *City Gate, Open Up*. Trans. Jeffrey Yang. New Directions, 2017.
Foley, Devon. "Suicide: I've Heard Its Siren Call." *Intellectual Takeout: A Refuge for Rational Discourse*. June 11, 2018. http://www.intellectualtakeout.org/article/suicide-ive-heard-its-siren-call.
Heyman, J. D., and Gillian Telling. "Carol Burnett, 85, Opens Up About Her Daughter's Tragic Death: I Think About Her Every Day." May 2, 2018. https://people.com/tv/carol-burnett-daughter-tragic-death/.
Hill, William. *The Glory of Love* (song lyrics) 1936.
Lewis, C. S. "The Problem of Pain." In *The Complete C. S. Lewis*. San Francisco: Harper, 2002.
Lincoln, Abraham. "Letter to Fanny McCullough." In *The Collected Works of Abraham Lincoln, Vol. 6*. New Brunswick, NJ: Rutgers University Press, 1955.
Nelson, Willie. "Something You Get Through." Released April 6, 2018. Track 5 on *Last Man Standing*. Sound Emporium Studios, Legacy Recording.
Vance, J. D. *Hillbilly Elegy*. HarperCollins, 2016.

# Chapter 17: Once in a Blue Moon

## Christina Alise McDermott

I'm an elementary school teacher who teaches grades three to seven. I've been doing this for almost fifteen years, which is to say I am about half way through my career. Not a whole lot surprises me anymore. I have seen all kinds of students: happy, well-adjusted ones. Ones that are future candidates for the FBI's most wanted. Ones that are brilliant and inspiring. And ones that prove the apple really does not fall far from the tree. However, there are a few over the years that have tested my strength, perseverance, and faith in humanity. Annie was one of those.

Even though it was a few years ago, I recall her first day in my grade five classroom—she walked in, maybe four and a half feet tall, wearing a High School Musical t-shirt and these purple streaks in her auburn hair. Her hazel eyes were scoping the classroom and the other students, almost with a raptor-like quality. The first week of school is generally a honeymoon—students are on their best behaviour, wanting to make a good impression on their new teacher.

Annie sat down at a desk near some other girls, and began to work on the "Get To Know You" sheet I had left on all the desks. Everything had been quiet and calm, until just before recess, one of the boys bumped into her desk, knocking her marker across the page. She leapt out of her

---

C. A. McDermott (✉)
Salmon Arm, BC, Canada

© The Author(s) 2019
S. Steel and A. Homeniuk (eds.),
*Suffering and the Intelligence of Love in the Teaching Life*,
https://doi.org/10.1007/978-3-030-05958-3_25

chair and started screaming at the boy. The whole class, including myself, was shocked at the anger she exhibited for such a minor transgression. I moved over to intervene and Annie turned her anger on me, snapping "You can't tell me what to do!" Up until that point, I had never actually had a student scream at me. She continued glaring at me as the recess bell rang, and the rest of the class filed out.

I waited a couple of minutes, and walked over to her desk, ready to send her to the office. She looked up with a smile and said, "What do you think of my picture Ms. M?" as if nothing had happened. In the coming days and weeks, I would learn that this was Annie's pattern: small incident, blow up, calm down, repeat *ad nauseum* multiple times a day.

No teacher or student was spared her wrath, and often it was unpredictable. Never a rhyme or a reason: however, an explanation would arrive, often at the end of the day via email: "Annie had a rough night, not enough sleep," "She's coming down with a cold," or "Her mother dropped by drunk last night." These emails would come from her aunt who was trying her best to parent Annie; however, she had four other kids of her own, and the household was always in some sort of chaos.

Annie's father was living in Alberta, working on the rigs, and he only had five days off a month. He was well-intentioned, but after those five days he spent with Annie would come some of her worst outbursts. There would be days where she was incapable of being in the classroom for more than a few minutes at a time because of her anger. Annie's mother, on the other hand, lived in the area, but she had surrendered custody years before because of her addictions and inability to parent. She would occasionally drop into Annie's life, and that would wreak even more havoc.

Overtime, a routine was established between Annie and me: she would perceive a slight from a classmate; she would react, and I would intervene while trying to teach an entire class a lesson. Then came her inevitable explosion, and my escorting her to the principal's office. Throughout that walk, she would scream at me what a horrible teacher I was, how she hated me, and how her dad was going to get me fired. Occasionally she would change it up, calling me a psycho or a stalker. The whole time, I would manage to stay calm until dropping her off at the office; I would then walk down the hallway and have to pause and breathe to find my sanity and centre.

One day, while she was in the middle of her usual venom-filled diatribe I said, "You know Annie, I still like you. Even when you mess up or make a mistake, I still like you." She paused, took my words in and then started yelling and crying, "Liar! You are lying! I hate you!" From that moment on, every time she exploded or made a mistake, I would repeat, "I still like you. It's okay. I still like you."

It was the week before spring break when the school got word that Annie was moving and going to live with her father in Alberta. That week, her outbursts reached a fevered pitch unseen until then. It was one of the hardest weeks I've ever had as a teacher, and it was so hard to keep saying that I still liked her, even when she was spewing such anger at me.

On that Friday, after all the kids had left, I was sitting at my desk, exhausted, completely drained, spent, with nothing left in the tank. I was getting my things together, when I noticed a hand drawn picture, sitting on my desk. It was a picture of two people, one a tall brown-haired stick figure, standing beside a purple-haired smaller figure with a school in the background, and blue sky with the sun shining.

Across the top of the page, written in blue marker were the words, "Ms. M you are the best teacher ever. I will miss you. I wish you were my mom. Love Annie."

Often as a teacher, you always wonder if anything you've said, done or taught made a difference. You don't find out the impact you've had on a student, until 15–20 years later when a former student will come up to you. Once in a blue moon, it's a little bit sooner.

# Index

**A**
Ableism, 102, 103, 106, 107, 109
Aeschylus, 3, 16
*Aidos* ("shame" or "awe"), 61, 107, 126
Ajahn Chah, 14, 83–87, 89
*Amor Fati*, 128
Anthony of Padua, St., 145
Aquinas, St. Thomas, 25
Atwood, Margaret, 55, 58
Augustine, St., 35, 163
Aurelius, Marcus, 163

**B**
Bee, Samantha, 101
Benedict of Nursia, St., 137
*Bikkhus*, 90
Bloom, Benjamin, 30
Blues, 14, 73–76, 78
*Bot*, 85, 90
*Brahmacharya* ("chastity-of-spirit"), 32, 33
Brooks, David, 160
Brown, Daniel James, 192

Bruno, Giordano, 3, 16
Brutus, Marcus Junius, 31, 33
Buddha, 8, 14, 74, 83, 85, 90, 140
Burnett, Carol, 192, 193
Burr, Raymond, 104

**C**
Cameron, James, 104
Carrey, Jim, 103
Christ, 10, 38, 40, 44, 124
*Cloud of Unknowing*, 125, 130, 137
Comic books, 105
Compassion, 37, 39, 58, 65, 75, 146
Courage, 13, 34, 37, 42–45, 102

**D**
Dao, Bei, 191
*Darsana* (also "seeing," as related to theoria), 32, 33
*Dasanas*, 86, 90
Dewey, John, 9, 10
Dickens, Charles, 103

Disability, 14, 100, 101, 103–105, 107–109
*Dukkha*, 8

### E
*Ecclesiastes*, 193
*Eros* (desire), 15, 23–25, 27, 30–32, 34, 58, 76–78, 122, 125, 128, 129, 142, 146, 147, 155

### F
Family, 14, 16, 43, 57, 84, 124, 188–192
*Farang*, 85, 86, 88, 90
Fey, Tina, 101
Francis of Assisi, St., 137
Frank, Anne, 163
Franklin, Benjamin, 163
Friere, Paulo, 9

### G
Gaga, Lady, 103
Gandhi, Mohandas, 31–33, 35, 163
Gregory the Great, St., 137
Gurley, James, 134

### H
Hendrix, Jimi, 60
Hill, William, 188, 193
*Hind Swaraj* ("home rule"), 33, 35
Hitler, Adolf, 103
Hobbes, Thomas, 44

### I
Identity politics, 159–162, 173
Injustice, 4, 13, 27, 30, 37, 42, 45
Ironside, Robert T., 104

### J
Jewell, Geri, 102
John of the Cross, St., 120, 121, 136

### K
Kennedy, John F., 65
Kennedy, Robert F., 3
Kipling, Rudyard, 60, 61
*Koan*, 29
*Kuties*, 84, 90

### L
Leo the Great, St., 37, 38, 46
Levity, Daniel, 75
Lewis, C.S., 188, 193
Lewis, Daniel Day, 105
Libertarianism, 162
Lincoln, Abraham, 191, 193
Love, "the intelligence of", 8–12, 15, 16

### M
Maimonides, Moses, 27, 30, 34, 35
Mandela, Nelson, 62, 163
McHale, Kevin, 105
McKinnon, Kate, 101
Meditation
  samatha ("calming," or "one-pointedness" meditation), 24, 90
  vipassana (insight meditation), 24
Merrick, Joseph, 103
Montaigne, Michel de, 163
Morrison, Toni, 166
Muddy Waters, 75
Mueller, J.Z., 175
Murphy, Eddie, 101
Music, 14, 73–76, 78, 130, 139
Myers, Mike, 101

## N

Nelson, Willie, 192, 193
Nietzsche, Friedrich, 119, 121–130

## O

Objectivity, 144, 168

## P

Pain, 3, 5–7, 9, 13, 27, 28, 30, 37–43, 45, 73, 75–78, 100, 120, 121, 123, 188, 189, 192, 193
*Pakhao*, 89, 90
*Pansa*, 86, 90
Patch Adams, 7, 9, 15
*Pathos* (also "suffering" or "experience"), 4, 9, 27, 122, 123
Paul the Apostle, St., 138
*Peepahs*, 84, 90
Pieper, Josef, 24, 25, 35, 122, 130
Plato, 12, 27, 35, 37, 123, 130, 140, 163
*Psychopompos* ("soul guide," or "leader of souls"), 11

## R

Redmayne, Eddie, 105
Resiliency, 16
Rilke, Rainer Maria, 4, 16
Rousseau, Jean-Jacques, 163

## S

Safe spaces, 161
*Sala*, 84, 85
*Samadhi*, 85, 88, 90
*Satyagraha* (also "firmness in truth," "soul-force," or "truth-force"), 32, 33
*Schole* (also "leisure"), 6, 26
Shakespeare, William, 31, 103, 114

Shange, Ntozake, 102
Shaw, George Bernard, 54, 56, 58
Shinran, 8
Socrates, 37, 38, 43–45, 122, 123, 130, 147, 163
*Sunyata* (also "emptiness"), 24, 76, 88

## T

*Tathagatagarbha* ("Buddha nature"), 140
*Theoria* (or "contemplation" or "seeing"), 24, 32–34, 127
Thérèse of Lisieux, 140
*Tudong*, 88, 90

## U

*Upaya* ("skillful means"), 30

## V

Vance, J.D., 166, 191
*Visio beatifica* (also "beatific vision"), 24
*Vita activa* ("active life"), 6, 122, 127–129
*Vita contemplativa* ("contemplative life"), 35, 127–129

## W

*Wai*, 83, 87, 89, 90
*Wat*, 83–85, 88, 90
Weil, Simone, 144, 147
Williams, Robin, 7, 101, 106
Writing, as an activity, 6

## X

Xavier, Charles, 103
X-Men, 103

Printed in the United States
By Bookmasters